	DATE DUE		
REF.	REF.	REF.	REF.

D1072045

"Fantasizing is as basic to being human as are toolmaking and year-round sexuality. All the higher mammals play when they are young; it's their way of learning how to cope with the world. Little boys and girls do, too, and not just in physical games. They play with their minds. Since you are reading this book, surely you remember some of your childish daydreams and roles. You're luckier than most people, and likewise am I; we never quite grew up. That is, we never reached a point where we had no further use for daydreams. We're still learning. The universe is too big for us to settle into during a single lifetime."

POUL ANDERSON

Fantasy has enjoyed a terrific upsurge in popularity during the past decade. And during that time, the authors of this guide have helped virtually thousands of book-buyers in their famous Science Fiction shop. Browse through their *Reader's Guide to Fantasy* and you'll find the whole range of fantasy before you . . . from the possible fantasy of Bradbury to the pure fantasy of Tolkien to the terrifying fantasy of Lovecraft.

Other Avon Books by
**Baird Searles, Beth Meacham,
and Michael Franklin**

A READER'S GUIDE TO SCIENCE FICTION
(with Martin Last)

A READER'S GUIDE TO FANTASY

**BAIRD SEARLES,
Beth Meacham and Michael Franklin**

DISCARD

AVON
PUBLISHERS OF BARD, CAMELOT, DISCUS AND FLARE BOOKS

A READER'S GUIDE TO FANTASY is an original publication of
Avon Books. This work has never before appeared in book form.

AVON BOOKS
A division of
The Hearst Corporation
959 Eighth Avenue
New York, New York 10019

Copyright © 1982 by Baird Searles, Michael Franklin
  and Beth Meacham
Published by arrangement with the authors
Library of Congress Catalog Card Number: 81-69276
ISBN: 0-380-80333-x

First Avon Printing, July, 1982

AVON TRADEMARK REG. U.S. PAT. OFF. AND IN
OTHER COUNTRIES, MARCA REGISTRADA, HECHO EN
CANADA

Printed in Canada

UNV 10 9 8 7 6 5 4 3 2

This book is dedicated to Martin, Tappan, and Donna, who helped fantastically, and to Dick, Frank, Dawn, and the rest of the F & SF Book Co., who have been wonderful to The Science Fiction Shop.

CONTENTS

FOREWORD

Anthony Boucher was more than an editor, vast though his importance was as such to the evolution of modern fantasy and science fiction. He was also a writer, linguist, musicologist, political worker, churchman, gourmet, expert in the fields of mystery fiction and fact crime, collector of limericks, fiendish poker player, and endlessly much else, which includes being delightful company—and, often, literary critic. In his case, those last two attributes did not conflict. He never compromised; he would have panned a book by his own grandmother and praised one by his worst enemy, if he felt that was how the truth lay. (Actually, I do not know that any grandmother of his ever published anything or that he ever had an enemy.) However, as a critic he liked to quote the phrase "the noble pleasure of praising," and he seldom missed a chance to indulge in that pleasure and urge his readers to share the enjoyment he had had.

In the same spirit, I am glad to praise this book. It is not merely a monumental work of scholarship, it's *fun*. The latter is more important. Entertainment is what endures. Today none except specialists know the turgid romances that Cervantes satirized, but who among us does not know *Don Quixote*?

Please note, by the way, that the tale of the old Spaniard is not only tragic at the end, it is so, underlyingly, throughout, despite the high comedy. "Entertainment" need not mean "mindless time-wasting." I define it as "that which, presented, engages the attention and the emotions." In this sense, many of us who find the TV sitcoms a crashing bore are entertained by, say, Beethoven's last quartets or Hamilton's canonical equations.

Or by a good fantasy.

Look. Fantasizing is as basic to being human as are tool-

9

making and year-round sexuality. All the higher mammals play when they are young; it's their way of learning how to cope with the world. Little boys and girls do too, and not just in physical games. They play with their minds. Since you are reading this book, surely you remember some of your childish daydreams and roles. You're luckier than most people, and likewise am I; we never quite grew up. That is, we never reached a point where we had no further use for daydreams. We're still learning. The universe is too big for us to settle into during a single lifetime.

Not that I wish to claim any special superiority for enthusiasts of printed fantasy fiction. There are countless kinds of adult imaginings. They can range the whole way from a newlywed couple's planning of the careers they want and the house they would like to build, to the nearly metaphysical visions of an Einstein or Bohr.

Nevertheless, fantasy stories are a human basic. The oldest narratives on record are of this nature—*Gilgamesh*, Egyptian myths, the *Iliad* and *Odyssey*. With a few sideline exceptions (such as in medieval Japan and Iceland), the "realistic" story, nowadays snobbishly called "mainstream," is a rather recent phenomenon, scarcely noticeable until the Renaissance and not dominant until the late eighteenth century. Before then, the largest part of fiction was fantasy.

I even wonder whether human language, the very capability of language as we know it, originated in fantasy. A set of stereotyped signals is enough for most animals; why did our protohuman ancestors complicate matters? Facetiously, we can imagine Oom the hunter telling his friends about the big one that got away, and I have no doubt that this happened early on. More seriously, though, I can imagine those beings huddled together at night and wondering —fantasizing—about the powers of the tiger, the wind, and the dead. . . .

This is sheer speculation. What we have on hand is a solid, enormous mass of fantasy fiction. Besides, I remember a remark Tony Boucher made to me while he was still editing *The Magazine of Fantasy and Science Fiction*, which he had helped found. Judging by his mail, he said, a majority of his readers preferred fantasy to science fiction, but didn't know that they did.

This raises the problem of definition. Where does the first leave off and the second begin? I don't propose to go into that question here; it's ably handled by the creators of the present volume, and if my own opinions happen to be a trifle different, you can find them elsewhere. Let me simply suggest that the distinction is a business of degree rather than of kind—a business of just what form the writer gives the archetypes and how the reader interprets it.

All fantasy is fiction, in that it deals with events that never happened, people and places that never existed. All fantasy is realistic, in that it tells us something about the real world.

Moreover, fantasy is fun.

It's entertainment. Sometimes it hurts (*Oedipus Tyrannos* and *Hamlet* are entertaining), but always, when it is any good, it engages the imagination, the truly *human* quality of these flesh-and-blood machines which we inhabit and which inhabit us.

Enough Big Thinks for now. Let me proceed, joyously, to remark that out-and-out fantasy is once again on an upsurge. Not only is a lot of it around, but the market allows and urges writers to exert themselves to the uttermost limits of their talents. At the same time, we discover marvelous old stories that have been waiting, occasionally for centuries, to become part of you and me.

This is what the present book is for. It will guide you into Wonderland.

—POUL ANDERSON

INTRODUCTION
How and Why to Use This Book (and a Word about the Authors)

Some readers of this volume will recognize the three authors as collaborators on an earlier *vade mecum, A Reader's Guide to Science Fiction*. That effort was put together as an aid to readers who wished to explore as much as possible of that which is currently available in the rapidly expanding universe of science fiction; it grew out of our collective experience at The Science Fiction Shop in New York and the many questions asked there over the years.

The reader new to fantasy and science fiction might wonder what qualifications three people associated with science fiction might have for doing a guide to fantasy. More detailed information on the differences between the two will be found in the final chapter, but in brief, science fiction can be considered a subgenre of fantasy—it is that kind of fantasy in which the fantasy elements are given a scientific rationale—and readers of one are more than likely to read across the board and cover that spectrum that has high-tech s-f on one end and extends through the pure fantasy of Tolkien to the ghost stories of M. R. James on the other.

The growth of fantasy publication and readership in the past decade has made even s-f seem a static field; this is

13

just about the amount of time The Science Fiction Shop has been open, and the percentage of books of and customers interested in fantasy has increased by leaps and bounds. So have the questions on kinds and quality available, the components of the many series of fantasy, and a host of others. Out of those questions comes this book.

Certainly, one of the problems is simply finding the books. Fantasy as a separate genre is such a new phenomenon that the searching reader is likely to find, in his library and general bookshop, some fantasy in general fiction, some with the science fiction (if there is even that much categorization) and some with the juveniles. (Some librarians and booksellers still automatically consider *any* fantasy as children's literature!)

Speaking of children's literature, perhaps something might be said about that. For much of this century, fantasy was almost entirely confined to and considered as juvenile reading matter; enough of that attitude remains to make current fantasy aficionados still a bit defensive about reading "kiddies' books." Perhaps all that needs to be said is that certain books supposedly for adults are simplistic, immature, and downright dopey. Certain books supposedly for children are sophisticated, subtle, and universal in their appeal (even the children like them). More than a few of the books we touch on here are of that caliber.

In the first section of this book, you will find a listing of the authors whose works of fantasy are currently available, both old and new. Read it straight through or dip into it here and there; there's bound to be someone whose works you'd like to explore. Then you will at least be able to go to the card catalog, librarian, or bookshop clerk with authors and titles. Let this chapter be the equivalent of your own personal fantasy section to be browsed through.

The second chapter, "Ayesha to Zimiamvia," will give you the parts of the many wholes in fantasy literature.

But if you know already that there is one kind of fantasy you prefer, check out the chapter called "Beyond the Fields We Know, There and Back Again, That Old Black Magic," where you will find practically all the books mentioned in the rest of the text divided into the major types of fantasy.

Farther on, our "Seven-League Shelf" will tell you what

we consider the best of the old, the new, and 'most every category of fantasy.

Perhaps you feel that prizewinning works are the best gauge of quality. In "Half My Daughter and the Hand of My Kingdom" are listed those works which have been awarded the various laurels of the field, along with a brief idea as to what the standards for those awards are.

And finally, where did all this come from? What are the differences between the older fantasies and the newer ones? Or between children's fantasy and that for adults? What *is* fantasy, for heaven's sake? The answers to these questions are in an unpedantic profile of the field, which is the concluding chapter.

We have been told that our *Reader's Guide to Science Fiction* introduced a host of readers to a host of authors and books that they might well have missed. We sincerely hope this book will do the same. Certainly one of the greatest rewards of working at The Science Fiction Shop, if not *the* greatest, is that moment when a customer tells us that he or she loved that last book that we recommended. Perhaps, on a regrettably less-personal level, we can do the same here.

However, to make it a little less impersonal, may we introduce ourselves? Needless to say, all three of us have been associated with The Science Fiction Shop for all or most of its existence.

Baird spent most of his childhood trying to find books as good as *The Hobbit* and the Oz series—"long fairy tales" is the way he thought of them. The Science Fiction Shop was his idea; he is also a well-known critic of fantasy and science fiction, writing a film column for *The Magazine of Fantasy and Science Fiction* and a book column for *Isaac Asimov's Magazine of Science Fiction*, among other critical assignments.

At an early age Beth developed a suspicion that the world was Not What It Seemed, probably a result of exposure to *Grimm's Fairy Tales*. Realizing that the best way to enter Faerie is to pretend to be walking in the other direction, she has written several books (including *DiFate's Catalog of Science Fiction Hardware* and *A Reader's Guide to Science Fiction*) and has reviewed both s-f

15

and fantasy. She is currently attempting to write her own fantasies, and is quietly refurbishing the bottom of her garden in the hope of attracting suitable tenants.

In Michael's case it was a cousin who first gave him a copy of *The Hobbit*. Another relative advantage at an early age was a father who avidly read science fiction. Since then, Michael has read much of the work that's been published in fantasy. More recently, he has become interested in scouting out, reading, and collecting children's fantasies. He lives with a dog named Murphy and writes in what time can be culled from coping with the customers of The Science Fiction Shop.

And so, ladies and gentlemen of all ages, we very much hope that in the pages that follow we may succeed in sharing with you the joy and wonder that is to be found in those stories that make up the literature of fantasy.

CHAPTER ONE

Robert E.,
Howard Phillips,
J. R. R. & Co.

In this, the longest section of *A Reader's Guide to Fantasy*, you will find profiles of the writings of authors whose works you are likely to come upon currently, both old and new (further words on availability below). These profiles are *not* meant for the researcher—the information we want to get across is not bibliographic, encyclopedic, biographical, or referential. Our one aim is to give the reader an idea, a taste, of what the author's works are, and to do this, we hope, as readably as the authors we're writing about.

We have also tried not to be judgmental, a difficult task at times. Each of the authors of this book has written about those authors for whom he feels the most empathy; for those whom we most love and admire, some of that quality will inevitably show through. But if there's one thing that we have learned from the tens of thousands of customers at The Science Fiction Shop, it is the enormous variety of taste shown by an enormous variety of people. The masterpiece of one is the sleep inducer of another, and probably the only final arbiter of taste is time, whose dictates we have followed with the older works we've written about.

For the adventurous reader who wants to expand his horizons, there are two major problems: finding out about the books he hasn't read, and then acquiring them. As noted in the Introduction, "adult fantasy" (for lack of a better term) is such a new phenomenon that most libraries and bookshops do not have a special section devoted to it. Through serendipitous search of the general fiction, science fiction, and juvenile fiction, the reader might be lucky and find some of what he's searching for, but at what cost of time and patience! Instead, browse through this section —or read it straight through—and we find it hard to believe that you won't come up with a number of authors and titles that you want to pursue.

Having the title-and-author information at your fingertips is certainly a strong ally. If you're lucky enough to have a specialty bookshop in your area (there are quite a few now in the U.S., Canada, and England), they should be able immediately to tell you if the particular work for which you're looking is in print (available from the publisher). A general bookshop might be a little less knowledgeable, but could be helpful nevertheless.

Alas, the one thing we can't guarantee is that all the books we mention will be in print. Books, particularly paperbacks, go in and out of print with astonishing rapidity. If you find that your sought-for tome is out of print, the two possible answers then are to check out the library or comb every bin of used books you come across.

We said above that in this section we are writing about authors whose works you are likely to come across currently. That is almost but not entirely true. Because of the generally low regard in which fantasy has been held for most of this century, there have been some wonderful novels that have disappeared in the sands of time which one or the other of us have been lucky enough to come across. We have included a few of these, balancing the frustration of their unavailability against the hope that such notice might result in new editions of these "lost" masterpieces.

But for the most part, all these wonderful books by these wonderful authors can be acquired with just a little patience. So, as we so often say at The Science Fiction Shop— please feel free to browse.

LYNN ABBEY made a favorable impression with her first novel, *Daughter of the Bright Moon* (1979). The locale is an unspecified world with two moons, one bright, one dark, whose influences play an active part in this world's affairs. The heroine, one of those warrior-priestess types with Powers, serves the bright moon (hence, of course, the title) and spends a great deal of time, energy (physical and psychic), and plot battling the Dark forces, personified in an evil sorcerer. She is of a desert, nomad culture and also has some problems with the more "civilized" urban population with whom she must join forces.

It all bounces along with a lot of energetic action, and there are inventive details such as the telepathic horned horse who is the heroine's companion, and a rather blasé godlike entity who makes a brief appearance and almost steals the book.

The sequel to *Daughter of the Bright Moon* is *The Black Flame* (unfortunately also the title of one of the classics of science fiction, by Stanley Weinbaum), and it carries on in much the same vein.

RICHARD ADAMS caused a sensation with his first novel, *Watership Down*, a best-selling sensation at that. Until then he had been a British civil servant, an Assistant Secretary for the Department of the Environment, which of course shows in this novel of a rabbit society in an extremely naturalistic setting, the downs of England.

Its similarity to the works of the Hungarian writer, Felix Salten (author of *Bambi*), escaped most people's notice, but where Salten had mostly portrayed the day-to-day existence of his beasts in the wild, Adams provided a more epic theme, that of the search of a group of rabbits for a safe home, as well as a sort of fantasy within a fantasy, the mythology of the leporid culture. There is also a healthy dose of satiric allegory, which fortunately does not dominate the novel.

With *Shardik*, Adams essayed a human society, but of no identifiable place or time in history. Its major character is an enormous bear, portrayed entirely realistically.

In *The Plague Dogs*, he again returned to sentient animals, this time domesticated ones used in medical experiments. It proved to be strong stuff, a little too strong for his more squeamish readers. (b. 1920)

It is somehow fitting that JOAN AIKEN, daughter of poet Conrad Aiken, was born in a house haunted by an astrologer. Growing up in an atmosphere of mysteriously rattling typewriter keys and tossed vases as well as verses may account for her wild and wonderful imagination. Aiken is prolific, writing gothic novels, poetry, plays for children, fairy tales, fantasy, and things just plain strange.

Aiken is best known in the fantasy field for what could be classified as a "children's" series, but the imagination, humor, and quality of writing make them fun for any adult. The "Alternate England Series" takes place in a world wherein the Stuarts were never ousted from the throne by Parliament; the Stuart king is a good guy and there are Hanoverian plots in abundance. Beginning with *The Wolves of Willoughby Chase*, the series weaves a circuitous route through coincidence, kidnappings, rescues, reunions, and foul play by the villains. The delight is in Aiken's style, darkly Dickensian, and in her humor, witty and warm.

She is, as well, a superb writer of fairy tales, having several collections to her credit. There's a touch of Grimm in a lot of them, though she does get wacky with some, such as the John Sculpin stories, in which a none-too-bright country boy is constantly bedeviled by witches, or the tales of the Armitage family—on her honeymoon Mrs. Armitage wished for two children who would never be bored. She certainly gets her wish. These stories and others can be found in *All But a Few, More Than You Bargained For, A Harp of Fishbones and Other Stories*, and in other collections.

In a much stranger vein are the stories in *A Bundle of Nerves* and *A Touch of Chill*. "Cricket" is a quiet little story about a quiet little bunch of people—who just happen to have someone trapped in the septic tank. "Do You Dig Grieg" tells of a musician who will go to the ends of the Earth, or to its middle, for a little peace and quiet in which to compose. There is also some lovely romance in stories such as "Sonata for Harp and Bicycle," about a haunted, haunting couple and a mistake rectified, or in "Postman's Knock," which begins: "It all began when Marilyn, feeling about in the post-office box to make sure her parcel had fallen through, found her hand taken in a warm, firm clasp, and a pair of lips gently, yet ardently pressed against it." The story continues with a couple just made for each other and an unusual place to live happily ever after.

For the reader, adult or child, who enjoys quality writing, exciting imagination, and a slightly skewed sense of humor, Aiken is one of the best. (b. 1924)

A certain type of juvenile fantasy seems to come predominantly from British authors, but LLOYD ALEXANDER is a notable American exception. Though his fiction can be classed as "children's," the wit, humor, and quality of the writing and characterization make it enjoyable for most adults.

Alexander's major work is a series, the "Chronicles of Prydain" (named for the mythical kingdom in which it takes place), based loosely on Welsh and other Celtic mythologies. They tell the story of Taran, an Assistant Pig-Keeper, who's also an orphan and who wants to be a hero. Taran has been raised by an enchanter named Dallben on a small farm, and longs to leave to do valorous deeds. In the first book, *The Book of Three*, most of the characters of the series are introduced: Hen Wen, the oracular pig; Flewddur Fflam, bard; Gurgi, who's a person or thing that reminds one of an animate bundle of rags; and Princess Eilonwy, a vivacious heroine with a sharp mind, and tongue to match. Through the first three books, Taran quests for glory and finds that being a hero is mostly sleeping on hard ground. Also through these three the power of Arawn, Lord of Death, is building over the land. *Taran Wanderer* and *The High King* continue with Taran's search for his parentage, and the final battle with Arawn. There is a lovely feel to these novels, almost as if Alexander were writing the Mabinogion (a classic collection of Welsh mythology) for a very high quality animated feature. Prydain is a nice place to be, full of light and color,

21

but spiced with danger to body and soul. *The Foundling* is a collection of short stories that fill in nooks and crannies in the history of Prydain.

Alexander is also author of short stories and novels not set in Prydain, and while not as powerful as the series, they are infused with the same humor and warmth. Particularly good is *The Cat Who Wanted to Be a Man*, story of Lionel, who asks his wizard master to turn him to a human. Lionel retains many of his cat values, and his reaction to human folly, perfidy, and love make up the plot.

Simply put, Alexander is a captivating writer whose "children's" fantasy is quality reading for people of any age. (b. 1924)

Hamlet was not the only melancholy Dane. If you think of the stories of HANS CHRISTIAN ANDERSEN as sweet little tales for kiddies, or associate him only with Danny Kaye singing about anthropomorphic inchworms, think again. Adults who have never read Andersen, or for whom his stories are buried in the mists of childhood, are in for a surprise (and a bit of a shock) on reading his work. It is darkly shaded, often moving, often frightening, with an unnerving use of sophisticated violence (as opposed to the straightforward use of brutality in folk tales). Over all is a pervasive sadness of loss (of love, as in "The Little Mermaid," or of existence itself, as in "The Fir Tree" and "The Steadfast Tin Soldier"). The longer stories, principally "The Snow Queen" and "The Marsh King's Daughter," are real masterpieces of fantasy. Andersen was a true creative artist, rather than a collector like the Brothers Grimm. But in reading him, expect a moist eye more often than a hearty laugh. (1805–1875)

POUL ANDERSON's fantasies grow out of the Scandinavian mythic tradition, firmly rooted in the twilight time of the sagas, when folk memories of glorious heroes and capricious Northern deities clashed with the new god of the Christians. Perhaps it is the inherent music of the Nordic names and words, the powerful rhythms of the sagas themselves, or possibly because this is Anderson's own cultural heritage, but in these fantasies he achieves his peak as a writer. From the careless, immortal elvish folk, caught in a changing world, and the tragic, magnificent humans trapped in tales not of their making and out of their control, Anderson weaves complex stories of victory and despair worthy of the Norns themselves.

The Broken Sword is one of his earliest novels, and remains one of his best. It is the story of Skafloc the changeling, a human child stolen by an elven lord and enmeshed in the long war between the Aesir and the Jotun. The starlit landscape abounds with elves, trolls, giants, gods, and demons, and mortal men are used and controlled lest they discover their power to destroy even the immortal realms.

A changeling of a different sort figures in *Three Hearts and Three Lions*, in which a modern man is transported to another time-stream to take his place as the central figure in a great combat between the gods. He finds the sleeping hero in himself, and awakes the gods who seem, in our time, to sleep.

With *Operation Chaos* and *A Midsummer Tempest*, two novels that are obscurely entwined by a few transdimensional characters, Anderson left the long northern nights for the realms of logical magic. Both novels postulate an alternate Earth where magic works—and science doesn't, quite. In *Operation Chaos*, where the heroes are a werewolf and a witch, North America has been invaded and the mathematics of magic must be applied to learning to manipulate other dimensions and winning the war. *A Midsummer Tempest* takes the reader into one of those other dimensions, a world where, for example, William Shakespeare was not a playwright but a great historian, and the clocks indeed struck the hour that Caesar was killed.

In Anderson's fantasy novel *The Merman's Children*, he has returned to the north for his stage. In the thirteenth century Faerie has almost faded away, but a city of the sea-people still remains off the coast of Denmark. In fear for the immortal souls of his parishioners, a priest exorcises the merfolk, driving them away in search of a place where they can dwell in peace. The Merking's four children by a mortal woman, unaffected by the Christian spell, are left behind. They are torn between their mortal and immortal heritages as they seek by land and sea for their father's people.

In *The Merman's Children* there are no simple choices of good or evil, no combat in black and white. Instead Anderson has painted vivid portraits of two cultures, each having its joys and sorrows; the four halflings are faced with the necessity of choosing one life over the other—the reader must decide in the end whether he is weeping for joy or smiling a very sad smile.

Those who enjoy Anderson's creations should also try *Hrolf Kraki's Saga*, his recreation of one of the oldest known Norse sagas. Anderson has cast the surviving verse fragments in the form of a novel that captures the flavor of the original. (b. 1926)

PIERS ANTHONY's fantasy, like his science fiction, is well done, with a touch of the unusual. One of his earlier works, *Hasan*, is one that is most like run-of-the-mill fantasy; its use of Eastern magic, however, and the good characterization, lifts it above the norm. Hasan is a young boy, very gullible, and an evil merchant convinces him that he can make gold. Others are also convinced, and Hasan is kidnapped for his ability, starting a series of adventures that culminate in his search for a wife. The "Magic of Xanth" series also has a fairly young protagonist, though not such a gullible one. Bink's problem is that while everyone, and most everything, in the land of Xanth has some form of magic that he, she, or it does well, Bink has none. *A Spell for Chameleon* details Bink's search for his own particular form of sorcery, and for a loving companion. *The Source of the Magic* is the story of the quest for the source of said magic, and these volumes are followed by two more. These novels are a wee bit cute in their humor and may tend to irritate some feminists. In a different vein is Anthony's "Proton/Phaze Trilogy," a wonderful combination of science fiction and fantasy. The series begins, in *Split Infinity*, on the planet Proton, a strange world of the far future, but with familiar social customs; the rich are rich and the serfs are nothing. Stile is one of the nothings, but has a chance in the Game, a long-running and complex testing of physical, mental, and artistic abilities, about the only way a serf can aspire to citizenship. Stile learns that he has an enemy, a deadly one, and in his attempt to escape is shown the way to the world of Phaze, a land full of unicorns, were-wolves, vampires, and magic galore. As Stile discovers more and more of the rules that govern these two worlds, he finds that he has an enemy on both and a destiny on at least one. Too much detail would spoil the fun, so suffice to say that here is mystery, adventure, suspense, romance, and excellent writing and imagination. The characters, male and female, natural and supernatural and robot, are strong, interesting, and well developed. This is a good introduction to fantasy for the science-fiction reader, and vice versa. (b. 1934)

ROBERT ASPRIN's two books, *Another Fine Myth* and *Myth Conceptions*, tell the very funny adventures of a sorcerer's apprentice and his master, a demon who has lost his powers. The basic premise is that there are many "worlds," or dimensions of existence, and the magicians of each world frequently oblige their brothers in the art by appearing as demons when needed. Magic itself consists of the power to focus mental power and project illusions and to travel the dimensions and obtain alien technology.

The books are full of disastrous mishaps (the apprentice, Skeeve, accidently imprints a young dragon and is forced to buy it), absurd beings whose names invariably have some insulting meaning in other dimensions (Perverts, Klahds, Deveels, etc.), and atrocious puns (the best kind). Skeeve is hopelessly naïve, but learning. The sorcerer, a Pervert named Aahz who looks just like a green, scaly demon, is a tough guy on the make who has taken Skeeve under his tutelage, mostly because he thinks Skeeve will be able to restore his powers. The rest of the characters range from scoundrels to vicious would-be world-rulers. The style is breezy and cynical, and a wonderful antidote when the weight of serious fantasy gets too heavy to bear. (b. 1946)

Mary Martin is *not* Peter Pan—at least not the original version that J. M. BARRIE conceived.

Peter has a complicated genesis, making his first appearance in *The Little White Bird*, a very strange, partially autobiographical novel of a man in love with an affianced younger woman. Narrated in first person, this love is followed through the woman's marriage to another man and raising of a family. The narrator becomes a benefactor, and eventually begins to take the firstborn, David, for walks in Kensington Garden. And to tell him stories, one of which is of the boy who, at the age of one week, left his nursery and flew to live in the Gardens and never grew any older.

Two years later in 1904, *Peter Pan*, the play, was first produced, and two years after that the "Peter" chapters of *White Bird* were published in a separate edition (with wonderful illustrations by Arthur Rackham). Then in 1911 the novelization of the play appeared.

Peter Pan (a.k.a. *Peter and Wendy*) is an absolute delight for adults and children alike, written with a dark, even melancholic, sense of humor and a lighthearted bitterness at the cruelty of children, the wonder of childhood, and the world in general. (1860-1937)

L. FRANK BAUM might well be regarded as the founding father of American fantasy, in the same way that Edgar Rice Burroughs is the founding father of American science fiction. There had been examples of both from American pens before, but these two authors essentially (and needless to say, individually) discovered a new form, the series of volumes built around a land of the imagination. In Burroughs's case, the land was an entire world, his Mars/Barsoom. Baum's was a country, one that would take firm root in the world's imagination. It was called Oz.

There is something epitomally American in this multi-volume manufacture of entire countries—or let us qualify that by saying epitomally American of the early twentieth century—the America of manifest destiny and the faith that anything was possible. (*The Wizard of Oz* first saw print in 1900, appropriately enough; Burroughs's first Mars book came twelve years later.)

Certainly the mass-media promulgation of the famous film of *The Wizard of Oz* is responsible for much of Oz's fame; it is often a surprise to lovers of the movie to discover that there are over forty volumes about Oz (the number is officially indefinite since there were several privately printed Oz adventures). Of these, Baum wrote 14½ (the ½ is *The Royal Book of Oz*, which Ruth Plumly Thompson completed from Baum's notes).

There is more than the sweep of imagination that is American about Baum's books. There is a brashness, almost a rowdiness, about his characters, as compared to, say, the well-behaved elves and Edwardian children of contemporary English children's books. Baum's American children are hair-raisingly blunt—in fact, downright rude —to their elders; many of the magic characters are highly regarded because they are violently anti-dignity (the Patchwork Girl is a perfect example). Paradoxically, Baum himself becomes a little stuffy at times; he is prone to moralize, again in favor of early twentieth-century values such as hard work, initiative, and the idea of "my family/ country right or wrong."

Nevertheless, it is a safe bet that almost every imaginative American child of the first half of this century was hooked on the Oz books if they were available; an entire generation plus was inculcated with the idea of a magic country/world that maintained a consistency no matter how its geography widened. (Robert A. Heinlein, for instance, displays a strong knowledge of and nostalgia for Oz in his 1980 novel, *The Number of the Beast*, though his use of it might astonish other Oz lovers, not to mention Mr. Baum if he could read it.)

This popularity was severely curtailed when an American association of librarians suggested that the Oz books no longer be carried in libraries. This had something to do with their being nonrelevant fantasy, though one suspects it also had to do with the comparative rawness mentioned above, which was strong stuff by the insipid fifties. Dyed-in-the-wool Oz readers paid no attention to this, however, for themselves or their children, and as the interest in fantasy (relevant or nonrelevant) has increased, Oz has made a thorough comeback.

The majority of the series follow a pattern set by Baum in the first book, *The Wizard of Oz*, in which an American child is carried by accident across the lethal deserts that surround the magic country. He or she (more often she, surprisingly) has encounters and adventures with strange creatures and people until rescued and sent back home by one of the benign powers-that-be of Oz. After several visits, a child might be invited to stay in Oz, and a regular American expatriate colony grew up in the Emerald City, headed by Dorothy as the eldest (save the Wizard) human, and Toto as the eldest animal from the outside.

A variant of this would be events purely concerned with Oz itself, as in *The Land of Oz*, the second book. Here our young Munchkin hero, Tip, escapes from his wicked witch of a guardian and eventually discovers the beautiful young fairy princess, Ozma, who is the rightful ruler of Oz. (In a socko surprise finale, it seems *Tip* is Ozma, magically transformed as a baby—one can see certain librarians being slightly unnerved by this.)

Each book added one or more strange and wonderful magic characters, and the later writers who took over the series eventually had a huge *dramatis personae* to draw from, as well as adding their own.

As noted, Ruth Plumly Thompson (*q.v.*) took over the series at Baum's death, and eventually wrote more volumes than had Baum. Later "Oz historians" included John R. Neill, who had done the beautiful art-nouveau illustrations for the entire series except the first, and Jack Snow.

Baum wrote other books that were not about Oz, but most of them (*Sky Island, Queen Zixi of Ix, John Dough and the Cherub*) were about characters who had some connections with Oz sooner or later. *The Sea Fairies* is interesting in that it reads like an American version of E. Nesbit's *Wet Magic*, and *The Master Key: An Electrical Fairy Tale* was another manifestation of the Yankee—no European of the time would have built a children's fantasy around a mere invention. (1856-1919)

Werewolves, unicorns, cemeteries, and Death; these are some of the things of PETER S. BEAGLE's fiction. *A Fine*

and Private Place was his first novel, started at the age of
nineteen. It's a lovely, if slightly depressing, romance that
takes place in a cemetery. Two ghosts fall in love and must
fight to remain cognizant of what life was, so that they can
remember to love. *Lila the Werewolf* is another love story,
this time between a living young man and woman. At least
most of the time she's a woman. In *Come, Lady Death* the
invitation is to a ball, and Beagle presents the reader with
one of the most interesting, and touching, personifications
of death in fantasy. It's a short work and is beautifully
written.

Beagle's best-known work is probably *The Last Unicorn*,
a funny, sad, bittersweet novel telling of the quest of the
unicorn for her people. Her companions, picked up along
the way, as should happen in a quest, are delightful. There
is Schmendrick the magician, who rescues her from a carnival, and Molly Grue, kind of a poor man's Maid Marian,
and a truly enjoyable butterfly. Written with humor and
compassion, this is one of the finer fantasies around.
(b. 1939)

There is a type of fantasy, usually found in the form of the
short story, which is difficult to define as fantasy, and
CHARLES BEAUMONT was one of its finest practitioners. This is the fantasy of the macabre, of the psychological, and generally has little to do with elves and fairies, or
even ghosts and ghoulies, concentrating more on the "fantastic" in the human mind. Most of Beaumont's work is of
this sort, and his skill at characterization, mood, and plotting was above and beyond most other writers in the field,
practically guaranteeing enjoyment for the reader who
likes this type of fiction, or for anyone who likes quality
writing.

For those who like their fantasy a little more traditional,
however, Beaumont also has treats in store: there's "The
Howling Man," whom some will remember from *Twilight
Zone*; and "The Vanishing American," a short story with
the feel of a Thorne Smith novel, about a quiet little man
and the stone lions at the New York Public Library; and
there's "The Dark Music," a tale of a schoolteacher, very

prim and proper until the piper plays. All of these are well written, peopled with well-developed characters, and highly recommended. (1929–1967)

JOHN BELLAIRS has written several fantasies for children, and one, *The Face in the Frost*, that goes far beyond such arbitrary classifications. His style is light and funny, full of puns; his brand of magic is lighthearted. In Bellairs country a good magician has to have a good sense of humor, especially when faced with serious wickedness.

The Face in the Frost is the story of two magicians, Prospero (not the one you're thinking of) and Roger Bacon (not him, either). They alone have the knowledge and power to stop the activities of a particularly nasty sorcerer who has aquired an even nastier book of spells. Their adventures take them through petty kingdoms, haunted forests, and evil villages; they must meet and defeat many evil creatures. *The Face in the Frost* is, in many places, a very scary book; some of the traps set for Prospero have a distinctly nightmare quality. It is also a very funny book, sometimes broad, sometimes quite subtle. Prospero's smart-aleck magic mirror is memorable, while the Latin puns and Bacon's spell for turning a squash into a carriage sort of sneak up on the funny bone.

One of Bellairs's series for children also deals with magic. These books are about young Lewis Barnavelt, an orphan who goes to live with his Uncle Jonathan in Michigan. Uncle Jonathan is a warlock, and his next-door neighbor, Mrs. Zimmerman, is a very well educated witch. Lewis and his best friend Rose Rita are entranced by magic, and by the delightful eccentricities of Jonathan and Mrs. Zimmerman. This fascination leads them into no end of scrapes. The series consists of *The House with a Clock in Its Walls*, *The Figure in the Shadows*, and *The Letter, the Witch and the Ring*. (b. 1938)

STEPHEN VINCENT BENÉT, a Pulitzer Prize-winning poet and student of history, consciously used fantasy to develop an American mythology, borrowing liberally from Washington Irving and Fennimore Cooper, Mark Twain and Walt Whitman. His most successful attempt was "The Devil and Daniel Webster," which has the ring of a genuine American folk tale. This spirit also imbued such charming fancies as "Johnny Pye and the Fool-Killer," which pictures Death as an old geezer with a rusty scythe, and "O'Halloran's Luck," about a leprechaun who emigrates to America with the Irish.

Writing in the turbulent era between two wars, Benét wanted to inspire and ennoble the American spirit of freedom and independence, as he did in "A Tooth for Paul Revere," in which a country lad's toothache starts the American Revolution ahead of schedule. As the war in Europe and the rise of fascism threatened to involve the U.S., Benét became an active propagandist with such stories as "Into Egypt" (1939), in which a young Nazi, sending carloads of Jews into exile on Christmas Eve, finds Joseph, Mary, and the Christ Child among the refugees.

"By the Waters of Babylon," a prophetic work about a young man who enters the ruins of New York scoured by an ancient catastrophe and dreams of its long-dead inhabitants, became the model on which many later post-apocalypse tales were formed. Several of Benét's most moving prophecies were cast in verse; his *Nightmares and Visitants* poems have dated only slightly in four decades, and "Nightmare for Future Reference" is even more chilling today than when it was first written. (1898–1943)

ALGERNON BLACKWOOD's name is singularly apropos —the very English "Algernon" almost humorously evoking a sort of Victorian sense of the order of things, followed by the sinister "Black wood," a hint of the Druidic primeval, the very *dis*order of nature which the Victorians feared above all.

In a way, that is the substance of Blackwood's writing, the rational post-age-of-reason man confronted by terrifying forces of the natural or the supernatural; Blackwood didn't make that much of a distinction between them— they were both powers pitted against the puny rationality of modern humanity.

Blackwood's novels have been mostly unavailable for

many years, but his short stories have been continually in myriad anthologies and collections. These short stories are usually a good deal longer than those of his contemporary, M. R. James, but his admirers claim, with some reason, that this simply provides for a greater accumulation of terror than the succinct James ever allowed.

The best known of Blackwood's stories are all typical of his works in one way or another. "The Willows" is about two men on a canoe expedition on a deserted stretch of the Danube (which is here far from Mr. Strauss's civilized waltz time). In a great swamp of willow bushes, they encounter strange and inexplicable forces (natural? supernatural?) that threaten their lives and their very souls. In "Ancient Sorceries," a mild and middle-aged Englishman is by accident (he thinks) forced to stay in an ancient French village far off the beaten track, where he encounters the active remnants of witchcraft (an oft-used theme, but this example, published in 1908, was certainly one of the earliest).

And in "The Wendigo," Blackwood transfers the ancient Greek idea of "panic" to the Canadian north woods, evoking the same response with a creature of Indian legend.

In short, Blackwood is one of the few masters of the arts of the supernatural story. (1869–1951)

Although primarily known for his science fiction, JAMES BLISH wrote two novels that earn him a place in the ranks of the best fantasists. *Black Easter* and its sequel, *The Day after Judgment,* are novels of magic—not Faerie intruding into the "real" world, but magic as it must truly be if one is to believe the grimoires. Blish's world is not too dissimilar from our own; perhaps, indeed, it is our own.

In *Black Easter* a bored munitions manufacturer seeks and obtains the services of a Black magician named Theron Ware: his commission is simply to release all the demons of Hell for one night. The cloistered Catholic order of White magicians sends one of their number, Father Domenico, to observe the experiment. The rules of the Compact that permit Father Domenico to be present also forbid him to interfere. As a result of this night of sorcery . . . But that would be telling.

Blish was as much a scholar as a writer, and applied his fine mind to research into the black arts for these books. As he says in his introduction, he did not invent any of the rituals or incantations contained in the books. He does warn the experimentally minded that in no case did he include the *whole* of any ritual. In addition to demonology, Blish reveals himself to be knowledgeable about medieval church history, and to be a credible poet in the Miltonian tradition. Lest all this sound too drearily pedantic, be assured that James Blish the storyteller never lets go of the narrative. Both books are plotted at a breakneck pace, and are as sensual and sensational as any novel of the occult. They are even, in a grim sort of way, funny (the passage where the U.S. military is presented with a computer analysis of the situation reaches for the very apex of farce). There is also a sprinkling of "in" jokes of the best sort, the kind that in no way distract the average reader while providing a giggle for the knowing.

(A note for fans of trilogies: *Black Easter/The Day after Judgment* forms the second book of possibly the strangest such series ever written. The first book is *Doctor Mirabilis*, a historical novel about the life of Roger Bacon. The third is *A Case of Conscience*, one of the finest science-fiction novels ever written. Taken as a whole, the series is called "After Such Knowledge," and attempts to deal with the question of whether the search for secular knowledge is inherently evil. The books are otherwise independent of each other.) (1921–1975)

ROBERT BLOCH's novel *Psycho*, with a little help from Alfred Hitchcock, sent thousands screaming from their showers. Although not fantasy, *Psycho* does demonstrate Bloch's ability to frighten. Working mostly with the short story, he carves small chunks of terror out of what seems a very real world, made even more so by his changing styles —dialect for one story, sparse Chandleresque narrative and dialogue for another. Many of Bloch's stories seem to be written for hobbyists—"The Man Who Collected Poe" is a story that will make a book collector jealous, but will scare any sane person, "The Plot Is the Thing" is for film buffs, and "That Hell-Bound Train" should interest railroad enthusiasts.

Bloch's longer works almost all seem to be homages to one writer or another. In the novella-length category, there are "A Good Knight's Work" and "The Eager Dragon," in which a Broadway type, à la Damon Runyon, tackles fantasy creatures, and the Thorne Smith-ish "Nursemaid to Nightmares," in which we meet Jory the Werewolf, Simpkins the Toothless Vampire, and others of their ilk. (These three stories are collected in *Dragons and Nightmares*.) Another homage, novel length, is *Strange Eons*, in which Bloch uses H. P. Lovecraft's Cthulhu mythos as if it were fact, as if Lovecraft had written not stories, but serious warnings. Knowledge of HPL adds to the enjoyment of this tale, but is not really necessary, as Bloch puts everything in chilling perspective. (b. 1917)

HANNES BOK was one of a few superb artists who drew and painted for the science fiction and fantasy magazines in the days when those genres were almost exclusively confined to their pulpy pages. His highly stylized, neo-Parrish illustrations brought to them an artistry and sensitivity new to the field of magazine art, and issues with his work are treasured collectors' items.

Bok also wrote, though his written output was sparse. It is primarily confined to two novels, one Merrittesque science fiction (*Beyond the Golden Stair*), the other a fantasy titled *The Sorcerer's Ship*. Bok was indeed an admirer of A. Merritt (though ironically Merritt's finest illustrative interpreter was the other great pulp artist of the day, Virgil Finlay) and *The Sorcerer's Ship* is in a way an *homage* to *The Ship of Ishtar*; in both, a man from our time and place is thrust aboard a ship of antique design in a world where magic rules, denizened by beautiful women and strange gods.

There is yet another "novel" (magazines tended to call anything longer than a short story a novel) that has never seen publication in book form (*Starstone World*); Bok also finished two fragments left by Merritt at his death, *The Fox Woman* and *The Black Wheel*. (1914–1964)

JORGE LUIS BORGES is an Argentine poet, scholar, and essayist with an outstanding international literary reputation. He is best known in the English-speaking world for his oblique and mysterious short stories which pose intricate philosophical riddles and often deliberately obliterate the boundary between reality and fantasy. These stories are available in several collections, including *Ficciones, Dreamtigers, The Aleph and Other Stories 1933-1969,* and *Jorge Luis Borges: A Personal Anthology,* with some overlap of contents. Borges is fluent in English and assisted in the translations.

"The Aleph" tells of an arrogant minor poet to whom it is given to see the *Aleph,* a point which contains all other points, from which all things can be seen. This story, perhaps deliberately, epitomizes a transcendent theme of all Borges's fantasy—that there are infinite layers of possibility radiating out from our own, each equally valid, which occasionally intrude on the mundane order of our lives. "The Aleph" derives much of its power from its ordinariness; the magic place is an old and disused cellar, and the poet gains no lasting insights from his precious revelation. All is as it was before.

The metaphor is made concrete in "The Library of Babylon," in which an infinity of books containing all knowledge and nonsense stretches out in all directions. The aged librarian of the story spends his years searching for the single volume which will encompass all within.

Borges's gift is to produce resounding effects through the accretion of small and subtle detail. "Pierre Menard, Author of *Don Quixote*" makes plausible the absurd lifework of a scholar: to find, in his own experience, the material to invent Cervantes's *Don Quixote* as his own, independent creation. "Tlon, Uqbar, Orbis Tertius" concerns an imaginary country that begins as the elaborate literary hoax of a few writers, and soon escapes from the reference volumes to permeate the real world. Each story is made believable by a mass of abstruse and contradictory academic footnoting.

Some of Borges's *Ficciones* are filled with rich yet somehow melancholy descriptions of the land of his birth. "The South" and "Funes the Memorious," in particular, evoke the strange, timeless magic of the South American back country.

Borges is not above compounding his own riddles with commentary. He states, unequivocally, that he is only one of the many authors, including Lewis Carroll, who wrote "The Library of Babylon." And he wonders, in an essay entitled "Borges and Myself," about the identity of the man who bears his name, wins awards, and is translated worldwide. The cumulative effect of Borges is sublime uncertainty, a kind of waking dream in which nothing, not even the dream, can be trusted. (b. 1899)

RAY BRADBURY is certainly one of those names that the general public associates with science fiction, but there is precious little science (high *or* low tech) in the Bradbury canon, and, when examined, the majority of his stories are fantasies. Even the famous *Martian Chronicles*, though they use the stuff of s-f and take place mostly on a world which Bradbury calls Mars, are a series of fantasy variations on a nonrealistic world, a bits-and-pieces parable about the rape of innocence and illusion by a spreading humanity.

Many believe that Bradbury's best work was his very earliest, the short stories of the macabre and supernatural that were collected in *Dark Carnival*, a book that is now so rare that it is a prized collectors' item. (About half of the stories therein are in a later collection, *The October Country*.) They're wonderfully evocative and succinct, such as "Interim," which is less than two pages long and tells of a happening in a graveyard that anywhere else might be called a blessed event. Another favorite is "The Homecoming," which concerns a sort of proto-Addams family; the protagonist, a young boy, is miserable because he is not a vampire or werewolf as is everyone else of his large clan.

Bradbury seems most comfortable with the short story, as the many collections of his work attest; even his one fantasy novel, *Something Wicked This Way Comes*, is episodic, but nevertheless chillingly effective as it recounts what happens as a small mysterious carnival opens in a Midwestern town.

When Bradbury's mannered style and his sometimes tenuous ideas work together, there is certainly no one whose writing is like his. Fans of his stories are unhappy that for the past decade or so most of his creative effort has gone into poetry and the theater. (b. 1920)

K. M. BRIGGS was at least as well known for her scholarly work in the field of fantasy as for her fiction; among her works of nonfiction are *The Anatomy of Puck, The Personnel of Fairyland,* and *An Encyclopedia of Fairies.*

She drew on her great store of knowledge of myth and folklore for the inspiration and texturing of her two novels, *Kate Crackernuts* and *Hobberdy Dick.* The first is based very closely on an old folk tale of the Orkneys, telling the story of two Kates, friends from the age of six and stepsisters at the age of twelve when their respective parents, a king and queen, marry. All seems well until the queen, jealous of her stepdaughter's beauty, begins to practice black arts on her. Queen's Kate tries to help King's Kate, but to no avail, and King's Kate falls prey to the spells of the hideous witch Mal Gross. Both Kates run away, to finally find love and a cure for the spells. Briggs's parallels with the legend are practically one to one, and she breathes length and life into this story of witches' illusion and fairy magic.

Hobberdy Dick details a period of time in the life of a hob, or hobgoblin, during the mid-seventeenth century. Although Puritan influence has brought evil connotations to these beings, a hob was actually a benevolent spirit, helping around the house and farm, usually repaid with a saucer of milk and a kindly tongue. Hobberdy Dick is the hob charged with the care and keeping of Widford Manor, and times are difficult: the old family has vacated and the new tenants are city people—and Puritans. This will *not* be a happy home, for the humans or Hobberdy, until it comes into the hands of the only member of the family the hob considers deserving of it, Joel, eldest son of the merchant owner and the only one to appreciate the country life and the old ways. The tale that unfolds, with Hobberdy seeing as his only chance that of playing Cupid between Joel and

Anne Seckar, a penniless country girl, is a delight not only for its humor and warmth, but for its feeling of reality, captured by the frequent use of consistent mythology and well-researched folklore. (1898–1980)

TERRY BROOKS was hailed by some as the closest thing yet to Tolkien when his *The Sword of Shanara* was first published. Others thought that he might be a little too close for comfort, but those that just wanted a fast-paced fantasy had a good time with this one, set in a world of elves, gnomes, and a Warlock Lord who tries to block the valiant band who are seeking the sword that will destroy him. (b. 1944)

FREDRIC BROWN was well known in the science-fiction and mystery fields for his twist and double-twist plotting, and he carried this into his work in fantasy as well. Brown's novels are of the first two genres, his fantasy being of the short and very-short variety. About the longest is "The Angelic Angleworm," the story of a young man who's digging worms to go fishing when one of them flies away, complete with halo. This one is a good mystery, too; all the clues are there, from the duck in the display case to the sunburn, and the reader *can* beat the protagonist to the solution. Then there's "Armageddon," in which same is averted and a young boy is spanked. Most of Brown's fantasy is collected in *Angels and Spaceships* and *Honeymoon in Hell*, but devotees of the *very* short should try *Nightmares and Geezenstacks*, 47 stories in 182 pages. There are nightmares in six different colors, a sad "Fish Story," a happy new use for "The Rope Trick," and 39 others.

Brown was fiendishly clever, and the twist in the story is sometimes in the last sentence, or the last word. Anyone who enjoys this type of writing is sure to like him. (1906–1972)

Celtic legend and song, especially from the time of the Irish kings, has provided background material for many fantasists. MILDRED DOWNEY BROXON has put a special twist on that mythology in her wonderful novel *Too Long a Sacrifice*. The book begins conventionally enough (if magical fantasy can be said to be conventional) when the bard Tadgh is taken to be the harpist and lover of the Queen of the Sidhe and a changeling is left in his place. For love of him, his wife Maire follows after, and both are ensorcelled in the timeless halls of Faerie.

At this point, Broxon's book ceases to be common and becomes exceptional. Maire and Tadgh are at last released from enchantment and returned separately to mortal lands—the all-too-mortal lands of Northern Ireland in the late twentieth century. Myth merges with reality and reality with myth as Maire searches for her husband against the starkly real backdrop of "The Troubles."

Broxon has written one previous book, a Viking saga entitled *The Demon of Scattery*, in collaboration with Poul Anderson. (b. 1944)

JOHN BRUNNER, though primarily a science-fiction writer, has, with his "Traveler in Black" stories, slipped into the realm of fantasy. *The Traveler in Black* collects four of these stories into a somewhat coherent whole. (The "somewhat" is an indication of the very nature of these stories.) They take place in the far, far future—or past—at a point in space and time where chaos rules and order is practically nonexistent except for the efforts of a being described only as a quiet man dressed in black. He wanders through his realm, the one man with a single nature, "he to whom was entrusted the task of bringing order out of chaos."

These are strange stories, subtle and many-leveled, speculations on the nature of cause and effect, and written in an oddly stilted yet effective style, almost Cabellian, that is beautifully fitted to the subject matter. (b. 1934)

In a field that is filled with series, JAMES BRANCH CABELL wrote one of the longest on record. There is simply too much for one to go into detail on all its ins, outs, ups, downs, and sideways; but, to be much briefer than Cabell, it is the biography of Manuel of Poictesme (an imaginary French province), telling of his rise from lowly pig-tender to posthumous prophet, in twenty volumes comprising work in many forms. There are novels, short stories, poetry, and even a genealogical chart of Manuel's family.

Style is the thing with Cabell. The whole of his work was written between 1905 and 1948, but the more available pieces come from the earlier end of that temporal spectrum, around 1915 to 1920. He plays with the Victorian style that was no longer in vogue at the time, that of the author cozying up comfortably with the "gentle reader" and adding his own commentary to the narrative, but Cabell seems to have his tongue slipped into his cheek. There is also, in most of his work, an elusive erotic bell ringing throughout the landscape. (This ringing was not so elusive, in fact rose to a veritable clangor in *Jurgen*, a novel that was censured, censored, banned, and made Cabell famous.)

Although Cabell is fun to read, a *caveat* to modern readers: his style can be a bit verbose, and it would be a good idea to take his books one at a time, rather than trying to finish the series in one long read. (1879–1958)

MOYRA CALDECOTT writes fantasies with a moral for what publishers call the "young adult" market, and, given the constraints of the form, she does a creditable job. The "Tall Stones" trilogy is set in a bronze-age Britain, where all the people are kind and loving, living in harmony with nature, and gently led by their priests to knowledge of the powers of the Earth. A young girl named Kyra, realizing that she is telepathic, seeks her destiny with the help of the village priest, who sends her off to the Temple of the Sun for training. After many adventures, she finally arrives, and is taught discipline and responsibility by the all-powerful "Lords of the Sun," the spiritual guardians of the world.

A separate but thematically related book, *The Lily and the Bull*, is set in Minoan Crete. Here the Lords of the Sun are opposed by a queen who cannot accept the death of her only son. In her madness she tries to turn her people toward worship of darkness and death.

Caldecott's philosophy—one is tempted to call it a religion—involves living planetary and solar powers, reincarnation, astral projection, telepathy, psychic healing, and a communion of the spirit which releases all the good in the human soul.

RAMSEY CAMPBELL, first published in 1962 at the age of sixteen and popular ever since, is also fast becoming one of the major editors in the horror and supernatural genre. His writing reflects primarily, in theme and style, his great regard for H. P. Lovecraft. Much of Campbell's work is suffused with the helpless illogic of nightmare, and the skill with which he creates atmosphere brings the dreamlike terror home to the reader. Short stories comprise most of his output, but several of his longer works deserve mention, among them *The Doll Who Ate His Mother*, *The Face That Must Die*, and *To Wake the Dead* (a.k.a. in U.S. *The Parasite*). This latter is particularly interesting both for its provocative and extremely well-written examples of out-of-body experience and for its two different endings; the American version is a little more positive in its epilogue. (b. 1946)

JOHN DICKSON CARR. "John Dickson Carr? But he writes mysteries." And so he does, but three of those mysteries are fine fantasies as well.

In *Fire, Burn!* Inspector John Cheviot steps into a taxi in present-day London and asks to be driven to Scotland Yard. Upon arrival he steps out of a carriage in 1829, in front of the original Scotland Yard. This is the time in history when the London constabulary was being established, and Cheviot, accepting what has transpired, sets out to show what twentieth-century investigative techniques can do to foil nineteenth-century crime. In this novel, and in *The Devil in Velvet*, in which a professor of history makes a pact with the Devil to enable himself to travel to the seventeenth century and solve a murder committed in 1659, Carr stunningly evokes the period, complete with language and customs, costumes and weaponry. The mysteries are clever and the characterization is of extremely high quality.

41

The Burning Court is a different type of fantasy, taking place near Philadelphia in 1929. Edward Stevens, a book editor, is on a train reading through a manuscript about famous murders and infamous murderers of the past. He finds the picture of a murderess guillotined in 1861, a beautiful woman—and she looks exactly like his wife, down to the detail of some heirloom jewelry his wife loves to wear. Then a neighbor's death is found to be murder by slow poison. And Stevens is forced, to his horror, into an investigation of his wife that keeps the reader guessing even *after* it is solved by the reason and logic of a reasonable and logical detective.

For readers who enjoy fantasy or mystery, Carr is highly recommended. (1906–1977)

LEWIS CARROLL is, of course, Charles L. Dodgson, a British author and mathematician of the nineteenth century. There's precious little that can be added to the millions of words written about Dodgson and his paramount creation, Alice, though no one as yet has ever succeeded in analyzing how the scholarly and relatively unsophisticated young Dodgson tapped into some sort of mass consciousness with the fantastic adventures of his heroine. Her journeys to Wonderland and through the Looking Glass are superficially just whimsical fantasies with the anything-can-happen quality of children's stories of the period, but somehow they have a mad logic of their own that makes them as convincing as any more coherent creations of the imagination. It is equally mystifying that Dodgson's only other major work of fiction, *Sylvie and Bruno* (which ran to a second volume, *Sylvie and Bruno Concluded*), is almost inpenetrable by the modern reader. (1832–1898)

LIN CARTER came close, at one point, to making the entire field of fantasy into "Carter country" through his extraordinarily knowledgeable editing (of fantasy anthologies and "adult fantasy" series of obscure and forgotten novels) and writings on the subject (*Imaginary Worlds: The Art of Fantasy; Lovecraft: A Look Behind the*

"Cthulhu Mythos"; and *Tolkien: A Look Behind "The Lord of the Rings"*).

He also writes fantasy, a good deal of which is unashamed pastiches of pulp adventure, where fantasy and science fiction were less separately defined. The "Green Star" series, for instance, takes place on another planet, but our Earthly hero arrives there by a sort of astral projection, a handy-dandy mode of travel favored by heroes of Kline and Burroughs (witness John Carter's first trip to Barsoom).

Carter's hero, Thongor, is Conanesque (Carter has also finished various fragments left by Conan's creator, Robert E. Howard, as well as coauthoring new Conan adventures with L. Sprague de Camp). Mighty-thewed Thongor spends a lot of time careering around an ancient Earth dominated by Lemuria, fighting wicked sorcerers, rescuing beautiful women, and generally carrying on the noble barbarian tradition.

The "World's End" series is another mixture of fantasy and s-f, a "dying Earth" setting for rambunctious adventure. And in his "Zarkon" trilogy, Carter essays another sort of nostalgia, the superhero in a contemporary setting battling supervillains with occult powers. There are also numerous single novels such as *The Thief of Thoth*, *Tower at the Edge of Time*, and *Beyond the Gates of Dream*, all calculated to please the fan of fantasy adventure. (b. 1930)

ROBERT W. CHAMBERS's writing career extended from the turn of the century to his death in 1933. Before that he was a successful magazine illustrator. Like so many writers of that prespecialization period, his output was not confined to any particular genre, and he was very well known in his day simply as an excellent writer of popular literature. He was, indeed; his short stories in particular are models of clarity and conciseness, but with an evocative quality that can be chilling without melodrama.

He is remembered, now, however, primarily for the book of short stories called *The King in Yellow*. Though considered a classic of weird fantasy, it is a mixed bag. The last four of the ten stories are realistic descriptions of expatriate American art students in Paris; one is a sort of prose poem; one is early science fiction, taking place in 1920 (the future, when the book was published); this leaves five that are really fantasy, but these five are certainly worth the book's reputation. Linking four of them are references to the dreaded *The King in Yellow*, which is (we hope) a fictional book somewhat like Lovecraft's *Necronomicon*, dangerous even to browse through (and how sly to name a book for a book).

Other such stories are scattered through Chambers's *oeuvre*, primarily in the collection *The Maker of Moons*. There is also a novel dealing with sorcery, *The Slayer of Souls*, and a delightful collection, *In Search of the Unknown*, revolving around a staff member of the newly opened Bronx Zoological Gardens and his adventures in tracking down highly unlikely beasties for same. This last-named work is a whole new side of Chambers, revealing a thorough expertise in the light fantastic.

Though *The King in Yellow* is considered a classic and has remained periodically available over the years in one edition or another, Chambers's work is mostly forgotten, which is unfortunate. Not only is he an excellent writer, he is certainly one of the earliest American links with the Edwardian English *fin-dé-siecle* writers, Wilde, Beardsley et al., opening the way for Lovecraft and Clark Ashton Smith on this side of the Atlantic. (1865–1933)

Almost a decade passed while JOY CHANT kept her anxious readers waiting for her second book. Her first, *Red Moon and Black Mountain*, achieved great popularity almost immediately on its publication in 1970; at that point there were very few fantasies available of this quality. The novel treads a delicate balance between being Tolkienesque and being original. In the best sense, it succeeds in both ways.

Red Moon and Black Mountain has a conventional opening, one that is familiar to all readers of (particulary English) children's fantasies. Three contemporary children, with a minimum of fuss, manage to slip into another world. And it is in this created world that Chant is so extraordinarily successful—it is both epic and beautiful, peopled with a diversity of races, such as the nomadic plainsmen, the Khentors, and memorable individuals, such as the Princess In'serinna, an Enchantress of the Star Magic. The conflict is with the Black Enchanter, Fendarl, and there is enough magic and action for the most demanding fantasy reader.

Nearly ten years later, Chant's second book, *The Grey Mane of Morning*, appeared; it was a surprise in several ways. For one thing, it was not a sequel, *per se*, to the first; while set in the same world we had been introduced to in *Red Moon and Black Mountain*, it took place in a far earlier age of that world. For another, there were no links with our world at all. And it seemed to be in an entirely different key, concerning itself almost exclusively with the nomad Khentors and their unicornlike "horses"; magic and its attendant glamor, so rife in the first book, are practically nonexistent in the second.

Nevertheless, it is an interesting complement to the earlier work, and the two certainly assure Chant's continuing popularity, even if another decade must pass before she produces another. (b. 1945)

Beginning a writing career at the age of seventy-eight is unusual, but VERA CHAPMAN, born in 1898, had her first novel published in 1976. Before that, Ms. Chapman was active in the fantasy field at least to the extent of founding the Tolkien Society in London in 1969 and serving as honorary president in 1972. *The Green Knight* was that first novel and served to set the style for most of the rest of her work. This book is the retelling of *Sir Gawain and the Green Knight*, a late-fourteenth-century epic poem, except that in this case she has chosen to make her Gawain the nephew of the Sir Gawain we all know and love. In this version the wife of the lord that gives Gawain hospitality before his facing the Green Knight is actually Vivian, niece of the nasty Morgan le Fay. She has been forced by her aunt to marry one of the bad guys and set Gawain up for his doom. This story is told from the viewpoint of Vivian, and in the other two novels of the trilogy Ms. Chapman uses this same technique, retelling in these some of the Arthurian sagas of Thomas Mallory from the point of view of one of the women on the scene. Be aware, though, that these works are by no means feminist in approach; feminine would be a better term for her romances.

Blaedud the Birdman has its genesis in a passage from Geoffrey of Monmouth, one of the earliest "chroniclers" of King Arthur, but this one is not Arthurian. It tells the story of Blaedud, a Celtic prince who discovered the healing properties of the hot springs at Bath. It seems he also had visions from a Bird Woman (who just happens to fall in love with him) about how to build the world's first hang glider. Ms. Chapman has a lot of fun with this, even ringing in the philosopher and mathematician Pythagoras before the denouement.

If very romantic fantasy is your cup of tea, by all means try Vera Chapman's work. (b. 1898)

B J. CHUTE's *Greenwillow* is obviously not a fantasy. But then again, not so obviously, it may well be. What it comes down to is that it's a wonderful book with just enough fantasy elements.

Greenwillow is a village with no particular geographical location full of delightful characters, most notably the Reverends Lapp and Birdsong, Dorrie (no last name; she's a foundling), and the Briggs family. Or at least most of the Briggs family is in Greenwillow. Father Briggs is a wandering man, called by the family curse, or cursed by the family call, to travel to the ends of the earth just because they're there. He does come back every once in a while, which is why the Briggses are such a large family. The novel is the story of Gideon Briggs, eldest son, who expects *his* call to come at any time and labors to set up a farm that will support his mother and family while he's gone. He's also trying very hard not to fall in love with Dorrie.

The wonderful thing about *Greenwillow* is Ms. Chute's style: the book is a joy to read, with very real and lovable people, written with a bubbling sense of humor and character. Technically, it may not be a fantasy, but it's a lot of fun reading and deciding for yourself.

No one, but no one, writes stories like JOHN COLLIER. Perhaps a special subgenre should be acknowledged, to be dubbed Collierly, in case someone else does, but for the time being it's a field of one. Loosely his works can be described as macabre; this means that they can be fantasy, but aren't necessarily; they are simply clever to the point of fiendishness, mixed with a touch of humor and even, at times, warmth (in a cool sort of way).

He first achieved prominence as a poet, which may account for his skill and economy with words. He is best known for his short stories, though there are several equally skillful and clever novels to his credit. The most renowned collection of his shorter works is *Fancies and Goodnights*; its two best-beloved stories are perhaps epitomal. In "Evening Primrose," a disillusioned young poet takes up residence in a department store, to emerge only at night to partake of its vast array of consumer goods. He finds that others have had the same idea and that there is a veritable colony living there; also, that not only department stores are so inhabited, but other establishments have their colonies, too, such as undertaking parlors. In "Green Thoughts," the staid hero encounters an orchid with the nasty habit of ingesting animals—including said hero.

Innumerable other such delights await you in the fiction of John Collier. (b. 1901)

SUSAN COOPER has created one of the finest series in the fantasy genre. "The Dark Is Rising" sequence, named after the second of five novels, uses mostly Celtic mythology, with a liberal dash of Ms. Cooper's imagination.

The five books chronicle the latest major conflict between the forces of Light and Dark. The prime protagonists of the novels are children, but these works are by no means limited to enjoyment by young readers. *Over Sea, Under Stone* tells of the search for an object of power that will be vital in the final confrontation. *The Dark Is Rising* introduces Will Stanton, an eleven-year-old boy who is also an "Old One," as the soldiers in the service of the Light call themselves, and sends him up against "the Dark Rider."

The third in the series, *Greenwitch*, works with the concept of the power of the Earth, "a force neither of the Dark nor the Light nor of men." *The Grey King* is the fourth novel, and in it, with the help of a dog who can see the wind and a strange white-haired boy, Will Stanton searches the Welsh hill country for the golden harp that will wake "the Six Sleepers" for the final battle. *Silver on the Tree* brings the myriad and recurring elements of the first four together in a phantasmagorical conclusion. (b. 1935)

The Englishman BASIL COPPER is living proof that the works and influence of H. P. Lovecraft can be successfully transplanted to the other side of the Atlantic. Not that Copper is a slavish carbon-copy; his many supernatural short stories are varied and effective. They are often anthologized and there have been several collections devoted to them exclusively (*When Footsteps Echo, And Afterward the Dark*, etc.).

His one novel so far, however, is remarkably Lovecraftian in form and flavor, and is probably longer than anything HPL ever published, with the possible exception of *The Dream Quest of Unknown Kadath*. Even this is not exactly lengthy, but sustaining that kind of suspenseful horror is not easy, and *The Great White Space*, as the Copper novel is called, succeeds neatly. It chronicles an expedition into an unknown labyrinth of caves somewhere in Asia, the finding of a great underground city, and more, much more. There is even the Lovecraftian revelation on the last page. One does think, though, that Copper must have been having his little joke in naming the expedition's leader Clark Ashton Scarsdale.

Copper has also added several volumes to the "solar Pons" series of August Derleth. (b. 1924)

JUANITA COULSON, a relative newcomer to the fantasy field, has written two novels which, though using most of the elements already known in fantasy, do present them with a touch of originality. In *The Web of Wizardry*, named for a group of good magicians who are opposed to an evil sorcerer, she has a young maiden who is not only beautiful but an apprentice wizard as well, and in *The Death God's Citadel* a werespell cast on one of the major characters results in some deeply personal embarrassing moments as he changes to a cat unexpectedly. But even with her slight variations, she doesn't toy too much with the traditional, and should be enjoyed by fantasy addicts hungering for another quest. (b. 1933)

ALEISTER CROWLEY, a notorious magician and self-proclaimed the "wickedest man in the world," wrote one fantasy novel in his life (although there are some who call his autobiography a fantasy as well). The book is called *Moonchild*; it was written in 1917, and is the original on which the present flood of "demon-child" books are based. *Moonchild*, however, is about the making of such a child, not the results of its arrival. A group of magicians (if not black, then certainly gray) determine that they will perform an experiment to see whether they can coax a particular soul into a child. Their method is to carefully select the mother, supervise the impregnation, and then provide the woman with the proper environment.

But war is breaking out, and a rival group of black magicians sees this experiment as dangerous to their own plans for chaos. Sorcerous battle swirls around the chosen vessel, as each side strives to control her mind and soul. Events mirror each other in the struggle for spiritual dominion over the girl and temporal dominion over the world. *Moonchild* is a most unusual book written by a most unusual man. (1875-1947)

JOHN CROWLEY hovers in the borderland between science fantasy and pure fantasy, effectively juxtaposing the conventions of both to create works of great power. In his first novel, *The Deep*, the setting is a fantasy-style Earth, where superstition and magic abound, and the world is torn by a war of ideology and royal succession. Into this maelstrom falls a glowing object from space, carrying an alien observer. In *Engine Summer*, Crowley refines the trick, casting what is unquestionably an s-f novel into the style and shape of a fantasy. Here is the basic fantasy form, a quest for self-knowledge, with glowing imagery and strange landscapes. Indeed, the protagonist himself believes that he lives in a world of magic and fated destinies.

But these books, each in its own way a powerful novel, dwindle to exercises in style before Crowley's awesome masterwork, *Little, Big; or: The Fairy's Parliament*. Here the stuff of fantasy is woven deeply into the fabric of reality—not general reality, but specifically New York City and environs between 1900 and 2000 A.D. The book centers around Smokey Barnable and his marriage to Daily Alice Drinkwater; a marriage that draws Smokey, confused but accepting, into the world of the Drinkwater clan, its history and its destiny. The family live in and around a huge house called Edgewood, a little to the north of New York, and their world is just a little different from the one that Smokey has known. Dr. Drinkwater, his father-in-law, writes animal stories for children. He gets his stories by talking to the animals—not the large animals, but the small creatures of field and stream. The family photo albums contain pictures of elves. Aunt Cloud reads tarot cards; she never can learn big things, only the little day-to-day events of her family. Grandfather Trout lives in a rock pool some distance from the house—he gives sage advice on occasion, but really doesn't like to be bothered. He was once a human being, but fish live forever.

Like all great fantasy, *Little, Big* grows very dark at times, the tragedies pile one on another until all that is good seems gone, leaving only a void of sorrow. But this *is* fantasy, and after the dark comes the greater light, and joy is all the sweeter for its absence.

In writing *Little, Big*, Crowley, a New Englander, has borrowed names and concepts from virtually every British fantasist of the last five hundred years (making for some interesting mental detective work on the second or third reading). Yet his usage is so original that the borrowings take on the aura of homage, a tribute to those precursors who laid the foundations for his achievement, and bringing the British magical fantasy firmly into the new world. Whether *Little, Big* is a unique work, the only one of its kind, or becomes a cornerstone for the resurgence of American fantasy, is for the future to judge. But the deeper in you go, the bigger it becomes. (b. 1942)

When AVRAM DAVIDSON finishes his sequels, trilogies, and so on, he will be *the* darling of the series-prone fantasy fan. As of this writing he has started three in very interesting ways, and it is promised that they will eventually all be concluded. *The Phoenix and the Mirror* is the first novel in a series revolving about the poet Virgil, who in this case is a magician and philosopher as well. He is commissioned to construct a major Speculum, or virgin mirror—one that has never had anything reflected in its surface. The high point in this installment of the series is the building of the mirror, and Davidson makes good use of well-researched alchemical practices in the writing. *Peregrine: Primus*, followed by *Peregrine: Secundus*, and probably *Peregrine: Tertius*, is a madcap fantasy romp in which Peregrine, bastard son of a king, sets off in search of his long-lost brother. The delight here is in the wisecracking and sometimes anachronistic humor of the writing and with the companions of the quest: there's Attila IV, a Hun with a minimal horde, an Emperor Augustus ("Stingy Gus"), Claude the idiot, and Appledore, philosopher and wizard. Also begun is a trilogy started with *Island under the Earth*, possibly to be followed by *The Six-limbed Folk* and *The Cap of Grace*.

Among Davidson's finished fantasy is *Ursus of Ultima Thule*, a well-written sword-and-sorcery novel, and several short stories, chief among them "Or All the Seas with Oysters," the title story of a collection and a reasonable explanation of why one always seems to have more coat hangers in that closet than one thought, and "Or the Grasses Grow," a lovely and chilling piece about keeping promises. (b. 1923)

Trying to encapsulate the works of L. SPRAGUE DE CAMP is somewhat like trying to encapsulate the *Encyclopaedia Britannica* (though de Camp's works have a good deal more deliberate humor). His interests range from linguistics to the highest-tech technology, history real and history mythical. His science fiction is fantastical, his fantasy is rational, and his historical novels and books of popular archeology are as intriguing as either. And unlike most such polymaths, he succeeded in collaborating with another person of great talent in writing works which have become classics of fantasy (or science fiction—de Camp and Pratt tread a very fine line between the two).

De Camp was one of that incredible circle of writers fostered by John Campbell for the science-fictional *Astounding* and its fantasy sister magazine, *Unknown*. De Camp published in both, but became regarded as the epitomal *Unknown* writer because his mixture of the fantastic and the humorous precisely evoked the exact tone of the magazine. Being one of the original writers of what later became known as "sword-and-sorcery," his works have a freshness which later hackneyed examples of that subgenre lack.

The Tritonian Ring, The Goblin Tower, and its sequel, *The Clocks of Iraz,* are fast-paced heroic adventure in mythical worlds, with always a subtle undercurrent of awareness of the silliness of it all, as if de Camp were saying, "Now, this bit is going to be the damnedest thing you've ever read—until the *next* chapter." And speaking of chapters, who can resist chapters with titles such as "The Butterfly Throne," "The Serpent Princess," and "The Smaragdine God" (from *The Goblin Tower*).

Needless to say, with that kind of output there was no one more suited to finishing fragmentary works left by Robert E. Howard and carrying on the Conan saga, which de Camp did with aplomb, ably partnered at times by Lin Carter.

De Camp's works in collaboration with Fletcher Pratt, while if possible even *more* humorous than his solo efforts, are also in a curious way more serious, more literary, if you will. While the *Tales from Gavagan's Bar* are the wildest bunch of tall tales ever told, *The Land of Unreason* plays hob with the squabbling fairy monarchs from *A Midsummer Night's Dream,* who are suddenly saddled with an adult and drunken changeling (due to a slight mixup with the milk for the fairies on St. John's Eve). But there are also moments of pathos reminiscent of T. H. White, and a truly heroic ending.

The four (or six or two, depending on which edition) Harold Shea stories are the despair of anyone attempting to sort out science fiction from fantasy. Shea enters other worlds not by magic, but by science (using the sorites of symbolic logic or a "syllagismobile," as he succinctly describes it); however, those worlds are worlds of fantasy, being based on various works of fiction or myth (Spenser's *The Faerie Queene*, Norse legend, the Kalevala, etc.). The results are sheer appealing chaos, guaranteed to bring a smile to the lips of the grimmest professor of literature *or* science.

The amount of knowledge of the most diverse fields communicated through their works by writers such as de Camp forever gives the lie to the idea of fantasy being merely "escapist," or worse, "mindless." (b. 1907)

SAMUEL R. DELANY is an extraordinary writer of science fiction who uses the ambiguity of language to create amorphous and chimeral futures. He has written one fantasy novel, *Tales of Neveryon,* a book of many layers, with elusive meanings that seem to hover at the edges of comprehension.

The form of *Tales of Neveryon* is a series of five related novellas, with a single character, Gorgik, at the center of all of them. Delany calls the book "sword-and-sorcery," but there is little swordplay and even less sorcery. Nothing really happens in Neveryon, but the world and its people change nonetheless. Some of the passages are pure delight; there is an alternative-creation myth, which explains that God created women first, and that men are the descendants of a woman who sinned and was punished. There are passing references to small rubber balls that appear in the city every year, are everywhere, and then disappear as suddenly as they arrived. No one knows where the balls came from, or where they go.

The appendix of *Tales of Neveryon* is Delany at his best as a semantic jester. It discusses, quite elliptically, the discovery and translation of an ancient document. There is some trouble with the translation, since no one is sure that they have the words for "male" and "female," "master"

53

and "slave," correctly; it might be the other way around, and if so the entire story changes. Quite late in the essay the reader discovers that the document in question is the *Tales of Neveryon* . . . and maybe one should go back and read it again. (b. 1942)

AUGUST DERLETH is primarily known in the field of fantasy as H. P. Lovecraft's St. Peter, but the role of prime disciple and promulgator was only one of many facets of this remarkable man. He did indeed finish HPL's novel, *The Lurker at the Threshold*, as well as several short stories, but he himself was responsible for well over one hundred stories published in *Weird Tales*, many under pseudonyms. However, his major mark was made outside of writing *per se*, as a tireless editor and publisher. As editor, he put together an astonishing number of anthologies, both science-fictional and supernatural. As publisher, he started Arkham House (with Donald Wandrei) to bring out a Lovecraft collection which he could get published in no other way (*The Outsider and Others*, now perhaps the most prized of all collectors' items in fantasy). Arkham House, still in existence, has over the years since that first book in 1939 been the premier example of a specialty publisher that has been both successful and able to make a considerable contribution to its field of specialization. (1909–1971)

GRAHAM DIAMOND seems to specialize in adding a dash of imagination to subjects and themes common in fantasy and making of them something unusual and original. His first novel, *The Haven* (1977), is about your typical besieged enclave, but the besiegers are thousands of vicious dogs, who talk and are led by a fanatic demagogue (sort of a demadogue?), and those attacked could well be the last remnants of humanity on a far, far future Earth. On the side of the humans are most of the other animals, also talking. (One of the major characters is a parrot who, when he wants a cracker, will give you the recipe and tell you how long to bake it.) There's action and adventure, and all the talking animals make it a lot of fun. This novel pres-

54

ages a series which follows the adventures of Stacy, daughter of *The Haven*'s protagonist, as she and her companions (a couple of wolves and the parrot) search the world for still more remnants of humanity.

Most of Diamond's other work, such as *Samarkand* and *The Thief of Kalimir*, are set in the mysterious East and make use of Oriental magic and wizardry. *Captain Sinbad* is also one of this type, and is especially interesting for the fact that it takes up with Sinbad *after* he has voyaged his seven voyages and come home to Scheherazade. (Yes, it is the same one, only in this case the lecherous king has stolen her from her betrothed, Sinbad.)

PETER DICKINSON was born and spent his early life in Zambia, then was educated at Eton and King's College, Cambridge. Upon graduation he began work as an assistant literary editor for *Punch* magazine. When he finally decided to start writing for a living he immediately began to turn out award-winning mysteries. Then, while having trouble with one of his detective novels, he dreamed the first chapter of the final book in a fantasy trilogy about the Changes.

The premise of the "Changes" novels is that at a detour in relatively modern history, the English turn furiously and violently against machinery of any sort and begin to revert to a life much like that of the Middle Ages. Although the last written, *The Devil's Children* is, according to interior chronology, the first in the series. Nicola Gore is a young girl who has lost her parents in the madness that is London during the first few weeks of the change. She meets a group of Indians (Sikhs) and travels with them across England until they find a place to settle. The Sikhs are not affected by the revulsion that has hit the English, and Nicola must act as a barometer for them in the political, emotional, and societal reaction of an industrial nation plunged into what is now, of necessity, a preindustrial life. *Heartsease* takes place several years later, when all who cannot stand conditions have left, and the English have gotten used to living without machines. Then, in the final novel, *The Weathermonger*, two children, Geoffrey and

Sally, escape benighted England to sail to France where they become part of an intelligence operation in which they return to their country and work their way to the Welsh border, where the disturbance seems to be centered. Magic comes into full force in this finale and the climax is surprisingly epic.

Although *The Blue Hawk*, Dickinson's fourth fantasy novel, also has a child as protagonist, this is much less a "children's book" than the others. In this novel Dickinson has created a complex society, possibly of a far future or past, or of another world, complete with an intricate mythology and religio-political system. The book opens with a ceremony in the temple of two of the gods, the reconsecration of the king by the priests. An important aspect of the ceremony is the sacrifice of the blue hawk, symbol of the god Gdu. Tron, a novice priest, has been chosen by ritual, and therefore by the gods, to be "Goat" for the day—one who is allowed to act on impulse, even to the point of changing the rituals of the temple. Though he had planned to cartwheel through the center of the ceremony, he sees a vision which he interprets as coming from Gdu, the god he serves, and steals the hawk. This act dooms the king to death and Tron to exile.

What follows, with the priesthood attempting to use Tron and the hawk as pawns in a game of political chess, is a fascinating story of a world where the gods take an active part in everyday living.

Dickinson's fantasies, as with all his work, are highly literate, with good characterization and an unusual sense of humor. (b. 1927)

Well known for his science fiction, GORDON R. DICKSON slipped into the fantasy genre with his novel *The Dragon and the George*, a pleasant excursion for his readers.

The book is the story of a relatively mild-mannered college professor of our world who must travel to an alternate world to rescue his fiancée, who has been transported there by an astral projector. (Though the opening premise uses a machine, this is a legitimate fantasy.) Jim Eckert is to project only his mind, searching for his loved one mentally.

Unfortunately for Eckert, his mind comes to rest in the body of a talking dragon named Gorbash. And his fiancée, Angie, is still a human, or "george," as the dragons call them.

This is the beginning, and Dickson continues with a very nice romp, combining such elements as wizards, ogres, and talking animals with just plain humorous characterization. All this is set in the classic "quest" structure and has a satisfyingly cosmic conclusion. (b. 1923)

STEPHEN R. DONALDSON has created in Thomas Covenant one of the most unusual protagonists in modern fantasy. He is a leper, bitter at the way fate and friends have treated him, and definitely not your typical hero.

In the first of the "Chronicles of Thomas Covenant the Unbeliever," *Lord Foul's Bane*, he is transferred from our world to the Land, where the people hail him as the reincarnation of Berek Halfhand (Covenant has lost two fingers of his right hand to his disease), legendary hero and enemy to Lord Foul, vile and vicious villain. Covenant, thinking that in acceptance of this place lies madness, refuses to believe, calling all a dream. He follows the path of that dream, which leads him through magic and adventure of epic proportion to a climactic combat with Drool Rockworm, finder of the ancient source of power, the Staff of Law, and summoner of Covenant to the Land. This first book of the trilogy ends with Covenant back in our world, but not for long. In the second book of the three, *The Illearth War*, though only a few weeks have gone by for Covenant, forty years have passed in the Land, and Lord Foul has unearthed the Illearth Stone, another source of ancient power, tainted with evil. Covenant must strive, still unbelieving, to master the power of white gold, which he has used before without understanding. (There is no white gold in the Land, and Covenant's wedding ring is still another source of power.) The final volume of the trilogy is *The Power That Preserves*, and in this novel Covenant is still searching for the knowledge that will enable him to control the ring. This search carries him to his final confrontation with Foul.

Years pass after Covenant returns to his world, but, with the time differential, even more elapse in the Land, ten thousand, and Foul is again gathering his forces for battle. Thus begins the "Second Chronicles of Thomas Covenant the Unbeliever."

These novels are strange works, full of bitterness and beauty, by a writer who is part poet. One may learn a bit more about leprosy than one really cares to know, but this is nicely balanced by the gentle magic and people of the Land. (b. 1947)

The ornate, art-nouveau fantasy of LORD DUNSANY (otherwise known as Edward John Moreton Drax Plunkett; he was the eighteenth Baron Dunsany) was the product of a writing career of astonishing longevity, extending from the first decade of this century through 1948; he died in 1957.

His exotic fantasies of mythical worlds were a logical progression from the authors of the Mauve Decade, but without their slightly forced sexuality. Instead, there was an even more daring use of fantasy. Whole stories and cycles of stories were laid in realms that had nothing to do with Earthly history or geography, and Dunsany's phrase, "beyond the fields we know" has entered the language of fantasy pertaining to created worlds beyond our ken.

He achieved enormous popularity with his stories, novels, and plays (he was also an accomplished dramatist, perhaps the only major one in the literature of fantasy); this bejeweled style was of a piece with all the exotica of the East being discovered by the pre–World War I intellectuals through the Ballets Russes and the ever-growing importing of art and ideas from India and the Moslem world.

There are innumerable short stories, all the very essence of concise elegance. Typical are "The Hoard of the Gibbelins," in which it is told how the Gibbelins, who eat, "as is well known, nothing less good than man," protected their hoard of wealth from an epitomal Hero (and oh, what a devastating last sentence that story has!), and "The Distressing Tale of Thangobrind the Jeweller and the Doom That Befell Him" (whose title alone should intrigue), the hero of which has an encounter with Hlo-hlo, the spider idol.

In another vein are his "Jorkens" stories, tall stories told in the Billiard Club, an establishment that is a precursor of Arthur Clarke's White Hart and Gavagan's Bar of de Camp and Pratt.

Dunsany's novels are to a degree a different cup of tea, or, perhaps more accurately, the same tea in a much larger cup. The lightness and irony that work so well in the lapidary short stories might seem to the contemporary reader to become cuteness and coyness in the longer works such as *The Charwoman's Shadow*. But there can be no disputing that *The King of Elfland's Daughter* is one of the great fantasy novels. The story of how, to bring magic to his people, Alveric of the Vale of Erl goes beyond the fields we know and returns with the daughter of the King of Elfland, and what happens then because of this, is ravishingly beautiful and literally wonder-full. Anyone who has read of the horns of Elfland will never forget their sound as evoked by Lord Dunsany.

No article on Dunsany is complete that does not mention S. H. Sime, the artist who illustrated most of his books. Dunsany and Sime are one of those rare magical combinations in which the literary and visual conceptions are a perfect match. (1879–1957)

To find the children's fantasies of EDWARD EAGER is an enormous pleasure for any reader who has grown up with the stories of E. Nesbit; never had an American author come so close to that English paradigm of coherent fantasy. The influence is obvious, Eager's children in fact often being admirers of Nesbit's books, but in one of those rare transcendences of imitation, his books are as delightful as hers in a slightly different key, that of twentieth-century America.

There are only five books of Eager's that are definitely fantasies, those that comprise what might be called the "Half Magic" series, and one other. The first of the series is *Half Magic*, in which, in the 1920s, a family of three sisters and a brother find a magic artifact which gives wishes in halves. The children are as likable and as sensible as any of Nesbit's, and their adventures in coping with the mathematics of wishing for twice as much of anything are hilarious. (The indignant cat that can only half talk is perhaps the funniest.)

In *Knight's Castle* we meet a second generation, two brother-and-sister sets who are the offspring of two of the children in *Half Magic*; the time is the 1950s. They have just seen the movie of *Ivanhoe* and read Nesbit's *The Magic City*. Thanks to an antique toy soldier, the cousins are involved in a slaphappy combination of both.

We are back with the twenties family in *Magic by the Lake*; the title tells all, as they find that their vacation home is by an enchanted lake. And in *The Time Garden*, the next generation is involved in some complex maneuverings in time due to the Natterjack, first cousin to the psammead and the mouldiwarp.

Perhaps the most extraordinary moment in the series occurs when the two families coincide at the same time in the same place, a desert island. We see the encounter from one point of view in *Magic by the Lake*, the other point of view in *The Time Garden*.

Two other books of interest by Eager are the connected *Magic or Not?* and *The Well Wishers*. They are as amusing and involving as the others, but the device here is ambiguity; neither the protagonists nor the reader ever knows whether there is magic or only coincidence at work, which may annoy the dyed-in-the-wool fantasy fan. There is also (as in Nesbit's work again) a touch of social significance.

In his final book, *Seven-Day Magic*, Eager returned to the unambiguous magic of the earlier stories with the wonderful idea of a mysterious book checked out of the library that both chronicled the magic adventure as it happened *and* caused it to happen; the various situations in which the young heroes and heroines found themselves all had various literary allusions (such as what could only be a pre-Wizard Oz).

Those admirers of the subgenre of fantasy in which magic creates hilarious chaos in the modern day will find no better practitioner than Edward Eager. (d. 1964)

E. R. EDDISON is one of the true originals of fantasy. His four great fantasy novels were published across the second quarter of this century, more or less, and while modern readers may find them rather ponderous going at times, there was certainly nothing quite like them before they were published, or since, for that matter.

The Worm Ouroboros is set on Mercury, but it certainly bears no resemblance to the planet that we know, and can be regarded as a created world. The novel chronicles the epic struggle between King Gorice, sorcerer-king of Witchland, and the heroic Lords of Demonland; there are great battles, thrilling rescues, ever-youthful queens, and mythical beasts. Perhaps what sets it apart from later adventure sword-and-sorcery is the epic, almost Homeric quality of Eddison's prose. One can hear it echoed in his nomenclature. Witness the names of the Lords of Demonland: Lord Juss. Lord Goldry Bluszco. Lord Spitfire. Lord Brandoch Daha.

The same quality is to be found in the "Zimiamvian" trilogy, which has curious but very tenuous links to *The Worm Ouroboros* and should probably be considered as a separate work (or works). To compound confusion, the interior chronology of the trilogy is exactly opposite to the order in which they were written (which was *Mistress of Mistresses*, *A Fish Dinner in Memison*, and *The Mezentian Gate*—the last was not finished at Eddison's death, but it was planned and summarized to the end and the summary completes the novel as published). It is generally recommended that the series be read in reverse order. It is so complex as to defy capsulization, but it intertwines characters of nineteenth-century England with those of the mythical kingdom, Zimiamvia.

Eddison's works may not be everybody's cup of tea, but it is certain that once read, they are never forgotten. (1882–1949)

PHYLLIS EISENSTEIN made her fantasy debut with tales of Alaric the Minstrel, collected under the title *Born to Exile*. Young Alaric was a foundling who discovered that he had the power to teleport himself to any place he had

61

once seen. Denounced as a witch and cast out by his foster father, Alaric is adopted by a wandering minstrel. But witches are hated and feared, and Alaric is in constant danger. The stories chronicle his search for his true family, who, he assumes, will accept him for what he is. *Born to Exile* is a light fantasy with little real magic; the powers of Alaric and his family are hereditary. Yet the land they inhabit is marvelously conjured, and Alaric's quest for self-knowledge in a hostile world makes a good tale.

In *Sorcerer's Son* Eisenstein spins a tale of high sorcery: the combat between a witch who controls the forces of nature, particularly spiders, and a deadly wizard, the master of many demons. Between them stands the witch's son Cray, whose greatest desire is to learn the mastery of demons. Cray apprentices himself to his mother's enemy, allies himself with the demonkind, and eventually returns to his mother's side. The book contains some delightful passages, particularly the descriptions of the realm of the demons and the habits of the inhabitants. And even an arachniphobe will soon be harboring fond thoughts of Cray's little eight-legged friends. (b. 1946)

Although HARLAN ELLISON is generally thought of as a science-fiction writer, many of his stories are more realistically classified as fantasy. This is not fantasy with elves and magic, but the deep, perverse fantasies and daydreams of the human mind, set in nightmare realms just slightly twisted away from our own world. They are fantasies of hatred and love, despair, revenge, and inexplicable disaster. Most of the stories have a futuristic setting, but the future societies are shaped by Ellison's needs for the story; true s-f usually allows a carefully extrapolated setting to shape the plot.

In "Paingod" Ellison explores the source and meaning of all the pain a person suffers in life—mental, emotional, and physical. "I Have No Mouth and I Must Scream" describes an ultimate horror: the human mind trapped in torment, with no possible release. These two stories are typical of Ellison's style.

In contrast to these is "Jeffty Is Five" a tender, almost painfully gentle tale about a boy who never grew up.

Ellison has been described as a savage writer—he is at least an honest writer, willing to bare his guts to anyone who will pay the price of admission. That price is admitting to ourselves that our souls are like swamps: bright flowers and teeming life, all resting in muck. (b. 1934)

CHARLES G. FINNEY is known almost exclusively by one book, *The Circus of Dr. Lao*, and it comes as some surprise to many that he has written anything else. He has, though he is hardly prolific; the fact that nothing else of his quite measures up to *Dr. Lao* (pronounced, we have on good authority, as *low*) should not be construed as criticism. It is a unique work and has gathered admirers from far beyond the ranks of fantasy lovers.

Certainly part of its charm and curiously widespread appeal is that it can be taken on several levels. A recounting of events in a small Arizona town earlier in this century when a circus arrives, run by a Chinese and containing the most extraordinary collection of people, animals, things, and gods, it is a wonderfully imaginative fantasy. The effect of this wild collection of curiosities on various townspeople—saddening, maddening, sometimes terrible—gives the novel a philosophical and psychological subcurrent that never interferes, and Finney's Dunsanian irony, wry asides to the reader, and use of what is sometimes pure slapstick humor make it a surrealistically funny book to boot.

But in all, the quality of *The Circus of Dr. Lao* is impossible to capture. There is nothing quite like it and it is, needless to say, highly recommended.

The Unholy City and *The Magician out of Manchuria* have something of *Dr. Lao*'s surreal quality, but the fact that they take place in a somewhat mythical China puts them at a remove. *The Ghosts of Manacle* is a collection of short stories, all well worth reading. (b. 1905)

After reading JACK FINNEY for a time, one begins to be convinced that almost any time "'tis almost fairy time." Finney is fascinated with time, and plays with it as a sleight-of-hand artist, sliding it between romance and detection in one novel, slipping it under a ghost story in another, or just flipping it in the air and seeing if it comes up heads or tails.

Finney is probably best known for his excellent science-fiction novel *Time and Again*, but the same humor and compassion, the same quality writing, as well as the element of time, are also elements of *Marion's Wall*, a madcap and bittersweet novel about a young couple, an old house, and a ghost named Marion Marsh, who leaves one convinced that she was alive, that she was real, and that she should be a Hollywood legend. The time element here is seen in the evocation of the past through Marion's personification of the heyday of Hollywood. Finney's sense of humor comes to the fore in *The Woodrow Wilson Dime*, wherein we learn that there is another Earth, or anyway another New York, and that the people there have Wilson dimes, Coopernagel nickels, and other strange coins, and that if you find one of these coins and buy a paper at a certain newsstand . . . At least when Benjamin Bennel spends *his* dime, he ends up in a city that is six months in his future and way off to the side in other ways—in this world the Chrysler Building is the Dr. Pepper Building and nobody knows about Cole Porter, to mention a few of the differences. Bennel's a bounder, lousy to his wife and friends, but in time he manages to come up smelling, if not like a rose, at least not like a skunk. And there's a wonderful scene at the bottom of a swimming pool.

Time is also the subject of much of Finney's short fiction. *The Third Level* is one of his collections, and the title story refers to a rarely found level at Grand Central Station, where one may take a train to anywhen. The contents of this collection and his other, *I Love Gaylesburg in the Spring*, include science fiction as well as fantasy, but all the stories are full of Finney's warmth and nostalgia, and all are worth reading. (b. 1911)

E. M. FORSTER is not an author immediately associated with fantasy, but his few exquisite short stories in that direction must surely be mentioned. They are for the most part concerned with innocence (which Forster equates with primitivism) confronting the hidebound English morality of the turn of the century (a situation he must have felt keenly as a homosexual in still-Victorian Britain), and being assisted by supernatural forces, often characterized as classically Greek. In "The Story of a Panic," for instance, a stuffy group of English tourists in Italy is disrupted and unnerved by an encounter with Pan; in "Other Kingdom," a girl's devotion to a small wood results in a repetition of the story of Apollo and Daphne; "The Curate's Friend" is a displaced satyr.

Forster's fantasies are short, understated, and wonderfully touching. The two collections devoted to them are *The Celestial Omnibus and Other Stories* and *The Eternal Moment and Other Stories,* and the stories are often anthologized. After all, where else can one find fantasy of such quality linked to a name so respected in English Lit? (1879–1970)

Action-adventure specialist GARDNER F. FOX is a graduate of the comics and the pulps (he was a mainstay of *Planet Stories,* that bastion of space opera) which might clue the reader into his style, which seems to epitomize fantasy for the fun of it. Even much of his science fiction is redolent of sword-and-sorcery (after all, there's not that much difference between a mythical kingdom and a mythical planet). The novels seem to come as fast as bubbles from a bubble wand (*three* novels about the Conanesque Kothar were published in 1969!), and have as much weight and stay with one about as long. But they're an easy fix for the undemanding reader, and significance has never been a *sine qua non* for fantasy.

Of his two major series, the title of the first novel of each tells it all. They are *Kothar—Barbarian Swordsman* and *Kyrik: Warlock Warrior.* (b. 1911)

Although PAUL GALLICO is best known as a writer of adventure and sports novels (he wrote *The Poseidon Adventure*), his books for children and young people often have a strong fantasy element.

In *The Man Who Was Magic* a young magician, traveling

65

in a doubting world, happens upon the city of Mageia, where magic is commonplace. Here he learns many things, not least of which is that magic without joy is no magic at all.

Gallico's love of cats, evident in nearly all of his books, is paramount in *The Abandoned* (also published under the title *Jennie*). This is the story of London's street cats, some born wild but most abandoned by their owners. Although the book carefully reassures the reader that all this is a dream, the story really begins when the boy Peter turns into a large white cat and is chased from his home by his own cat-hating Nannie. Peter is a very inexperienced cat and nearly dies; he is saved by Jennie Baldrin, a Scottish cat, who is willing to teach him what he needs to know.

Most of Gallico's fantasies have little real magic in them; they are warm, gentle flights of fancy designed to make a philosophical point, or impart a moral, without making a fuss about it. As such they succeed admirably. (1897–1976)

ALAN GARNER's earliest novels, *The Weirdstone of Brisingamen* and *The Moon of Gomrath*, are powerful amalgamations of Norse legend, Welsh mythology, and British folklore, set in present-day Adderly, Garner's home town in Cheshire. An amulet worn by a young girl draws her and her brother into confrontation with witches, trolls, and svarts (goblinlike creatures), and with the Morrigan, the personification of ageless evil. On their side is the magician Cadellin (read Merlin) and the sleeping knights of Arthur. (The knights remain asleep, but with them in the picture, even the darkest moments aren't so terrifying.) The writing in these two is rich and full of atmosphere and detail, and there are scenes which can make the reader shudder with claustrophobia, or chill in awe.

Garner's later work becomes more and more "literary," sparser and more philosophical, with less stress on character and more on mood, or even moodiness. *Elidor*, the story of four children who must save an alternate world through the protection of four symbols of power, and *The Owl Service*, which makes strong use of the Mabinogion, are examples of this style.

Also of interest to fantasy readers are two volumes edited by Garner, *A Book of Goblins* and *The Guizer*, collections of short stories and legends about, respectively, goblins and other supernatural creatures and fools, from Robin Goodfellow to Amerindian tricksters. (b. 1934)

"Unheroic fantasy" might be a way to describe the novels of the phenomenal JANE GASKELL. However, that description gives no idea of the lady's enormous talents of writing skill and imagination. But did you ever wonder what was happening, as it were, on the home front when the heroes are off battling monsters and magic and marching their armies back and forth across continents? According to Ms. Gaskell's *chef-d'oeuvre*, the "Atlan" series, what's happening back there is more interesting, adventurous, and downright hair-raising than the front lines.

The heroine of the "Atlan" saga is the Princess Cija (*Key-a*), descendant of the Gods and daughter of the Dictatress of a small kingdom located on an antediluvian Earth where dinosaurs roam and the Moon has long since fallen into legend. Cija, despite her exalted position (and her exalted opinion of herself), is carried off as a hostage by Zerd, the half-reptilian General of the Armies of the great Kingdom to the North, as he invades the equally great and even more decadent Kingdom of the South.

While constant war sweeps the continent, even involving the mysterious island-kingdom of Atlan, guardian of ancient powers and cut off from other lands by a belt of airlessness, we follow the adventures of Cija as she rises to Empress, descends to scullery maid, becomes a homeless wanderer, is raped, kept, and abused, bears three children to Zerd, her half brother Smahil, and an ape-man, respectively, loses one (not to death; she literally loses him in a moment of confusion) and generally has more perils than Pauline and more adventures than Tom Jones and Gulliver put together.

There is no way to convey the constant flow of imagination that creates the people, places, and events of Cija's five-volume saga. After every outrageous happening, the reader thinks that Gaskell will be unable to top that one;

then she proceeds to do it. The color and invention are slightly reminiscent of Mervyn Peake's writings, though in a much more action-prone key, and Gaskell anticipated by at least a decade the baroque wonders of Moorcock's *Gloriana* and Wolfe's "Book of the New Sun" series.

Gaskell was a prodigy with two published books to her credit by the time she was seventeen. *Strange Evil*, written when she was barely into her teens, takes her heroine into a mysterious world of sinister fairies and talking shadows entered by walking off a spire of Notre-Dame Cathedral. *King's Daughter*, her second novel, is like a preliminary sketch for the "Atlan" series, and in fact takes place in the same world. On its own, however, it is a rousing adventure story, coming to a most unexpected climax.

Jane Gaskell, thank heavens, is a prodigy who did not burn herself out. One can only wait in anticipation to see what next will come from her superfertile imagination to shock, enthrall, and enchant us. (b. 1941)

ELIZABETH GOUDGE is primarily known as a writer of skillful romantic novels with a religious undertone—some, such as *Green Dolphin Street*, laid in expertly researched historical settings. But her children's fantasies will captivate any adult with an admiration for the gentler examples of the genre.

In *The Little White Horse* (1946), Maria Merryweather comes to stay with a distant cousin and discovers the long estrangement between the "Sun" and "Moon" branches of the family. Lost loves abound, coincidence is rife, but all the complications of the family, even including the fishermen who live in the Black Castle on Merryweather Bay, are solved by Maria, Robin the shepherd boy, and Goudge's wonderful animals. Chief among them are Wrolf, who is a trifle large, maned, and oddly shaped to be the dog he is claimed to be, but who is the very image of a lion, and the little white horse of the title, which comes from the sea and is not really a horse either, because of its single spiral horn.

Sweetness and light prevail, but it never quite becomes sticky due to Goudge's humor and storytelling skill.

Linnets and Valerians has very much the same quality; it is reminiscent of Garner's *Weirdstone of Brisingamen* in its tale of a battle between good and evil in the mundane surroundings of a tiny village, but the elements of magic and fantasy are very understated and subtle, and not for the aficionados of the epic or heroic. (b. 1900)

In these days of "meaningful" fantasy, when every other animal is an allegory, KENNETH GRAHAME's *The Wind in the Willows* is a refreshing breeze. It's not that Grahame's creatures don't have human characteristics and comment on the human condition, but it seems to be gentle satire rather than heavy philosophy.

Probably best known of the characters, thanks to Walt Disney, is Toad of Toad Hall, a delightfully pompous individual whose adventures take up a good portion of the book, but there is even more to recommend the novel. Mole and Mr. Rat, along with Mr. Badger, are the other major characters and figure in what are the transcendent sections of the book. In the chapters "Dulce Domum," "The Wild Wood," and "The Piper at the Gates of Dawn" Grahame evokes exquisite homesickness, heart-pounding terror, and quiet awe, respectively. (Almost all of the editions of this book are illustrated, so it might be a good idea to search for one by an artist whose style you enjoy.)

Grahame is also the author of *The Reluctant Dragon*, the story of the poetry-spouting beast who would really rather not fight St. George.

These works show that bankers, as Mr. Grahame was, were, at one time, people, too. (1859–1932)

ROLAND GREEN, in the "Wandor" series, has saddled his hero with one of the most extensive quests in sword-and-sorcery:

Go and win Firehair the Maiden.
Go and win the faith of Strong-Ax and Fear-No-Devil.
Go and win aid from Cheloth of the Woods.
Go and seek these—the Helm of Jagnar, the Ax of Yevoda, the Spear of Valkath, the Sword of Artos, the Dragon-Steed of Morkol.

Go among all peoples and through all lands and against all who torment and distress men, wherever you may find them barring your passage.

Go then to the home of him you call your father and take up the talisman and watch, while Mount Pendwyr splits with fire and the hills and woods rise into the sky and are scattered to the sea.

Go then at last forth to battle, and smite those who come against you, with all your strength and cunning.

So Bertan Wandor is told by the Guardian of the Mountain. If he can accomplish all of the above he may be destined to sit on the throne of the legendary Five-Crowned King and bring men to peace. And so he sets out, master of the sword and servant to the present king, to find love, companions, battle, and magic.

Deathless prose these books are not, but full of fun and excitement they are, with swords and bodies flying every which way and Wandor happily galloping along the road to his destiny. *Wandor's Ride* is the first of this series, followed by *Wandor's Journey*, *Wandor's Voyage*, and *Wandor's Flight*, with other novels of Wandor's wanders to come. (b. 1944)

I say, isn't that H. RIDER HAGGARD striding down the nineteenth century, helmeted in pith and with a safari of native bearers bringing up the rear?

Haggard is probably best remembered as a chronicler of African adventure in Victorian times, but his work amounts to far, far more than that. Africa was certainly his turf, but any unexplored corner of the globe would do as a setting, for instance Central America (*Heart of the World*), Tibet (*Ayesha*), or Mexico (*Montezuma's Daughter*). And while almost all of his novels are today regarded as fantasy, in their own time they were much closer to being science fiction. Strange beings living in odd corners of the world have been storytellers' material since the time of the Pharaohs, but in place of the fantastical, such as Swift's Lilliputians, Haggard, with the "lost race" theme, was legitimately speculating in anthropology and geography. Certainly, given the blank spots on the maps of his time, there could well have been remnants of ancient civilizations still lurking about.

Also at that time, mysticism and science were much closer together. Such matters as reincarnation (an idea often used by Haggard) were still legitimate subjects of research. And the occult talents of the immortal *She* would have been regarded in that day as far more likely than the atomic bomb. (Many readers do not realize that there are four novels about Ayesha, She-Who-Must-Be-Obeyed: *Wisdom's Daughter*, *She and Allan*, *She*, and *Ayesha, the Return of She*. *She* is one of Haggard's two best-known books; the other is, of course, *King Solomon's Mines*, which introduced his other most famous character, Allan Quatermain. This is the Allan of *She and Allan*, and the meeting of these two in that book is both pyrotechnical and unexpectedly comic, since neither is about to put up with any nonsense from the other.)

Haggard had an immeasurable effect on American science fiction through Edgar Rice Burroughs, with *his* multitude of lost races; as a matter of fact, John Carter first arrived on Mars by Haggardesque occult means. And Burroughs went on to imprint his pattern of action-adventure on American science fiction for half a century.

However one might want to categorize Haggard's works, though, they are as enjoyable today as when they were first published. Literate but hardly heavyweight, action-filled but not mindless, his many novels will continue to delight readers for years to come. (1856–1925)

Fantasies have been based on the mythologies, religions, and histories of many cultures and races, but ISIDORE HAIBLUM is one of the few writers who have produced Yiddish fantasy. Most of Mr. Haiblum's work is science fiction, but, though there's talk in *The Tsaddik of the Seven Wonders* about leaks in the universe and other such things, *we* know that it's magic that wins the day. Besides the Tsaddik's magic, there are several alternate worlds (past, future, and sideways), Jewish history, a little nice romance, and a *schmear* of ethnic humor. Part of the enjoyment of this book is the Yiddish words sprinkled throughout, but even the most gentile of people should be able to get most of them from the context. So—you should live and be well, and enjoy this book. (b. 1935)

LINDA HALDEMAN. In her first excursion into the world of fantasy Ms. Haldeman based a story on a painting. In the Tate Gallery in London hangs "The Fairy Feller's Master Stroke," by Victorian artist Richard Dadd. It is a fascinating portrayal of a scene from Faerie.

The Lastborn of Elvinwood begins with a problem for the fairies of England's Elvinwood—the race is dying out and needs an infusion of new blood—and runs merrily along to a climax pictured by Dadd so many years ago. Standard characters and elements of British mythology dot the landscape of this novel: changelings and spells, Oberon, Titania, and even Merlin, but Haldeman brings them to new life with a wit and humor that is all her own. *Lastborn* is a delightful melding of age-old legends with modern times.

Another fantasy, in a slightly different vein, is *Star of the Sea*, a quiet, simple tale about a lonely little girl, a statue, and a few small miracles. Here, as in the above-mentioned novel, there are humor, charm, and wit. *Esbae*, Ms. Haldeman's third novel, is the story of a spirit, and a demon, and love, and a puppy. In this book, even more than in the previous two, she demonstrates her amazing ability to introduce magic (and it's real—none of this psychological stuff) into the everyday, even mundane, world.

NEIL HANCOCK's entrance to the fantasy field was in 1977 with a series almost as epic in proportion as J. R. R. Tolkien's trilogy. In fact, there are many similarities in theme and structure, but Mr. Hancock's work, the "Circle of Light" tetralogy, could not really be called unoriginal. Using the quest structure, he produces his first switch by giving his main character leads to an otter, a bear, an elf, a dwarf, and two rustic humans. These six, chosen as bearers of a talisman, the Arkenchest, must contend, aided by the wizards of the Circle of Light, with the Queen of the Dark to save their world. Though likenesses may be found with many major novels of fantasy, the setting of these novels and Hancock's characterizations of the animals make for an enjoyable adventure.

Dragon Winter, an almost allegorical novel (but still light enough to be fun), also makes good use of animals as characters.

PAUL HAZEL has drawn together the oldest myths and legends of Ireland and Britain to create a primeval saga of kingship at the dawn of history. The first book of the "Finnbranch" (what Hazel calls the trilogy) is *Yearwood* (1980). Deep in the mountain fastness of Morrigan, seated between the twin peaks of Gear Finn, dwell the women of the Kell, the old people who still cling to the worship of the goddess Anu. In this household lives a young boy: nameless, for his mother will not name him, and a bastard, for she will not reveal who his father was. From the first words of the book ...

My Mother and her women are of the bitter lineage of the Selchie, the spawn of sealmen and shore folk. In their blood the memory of the undersea kingdoms still rages. ...

the reader knows that to enter this world is to walk in a land of dreams and magic, where life is as sweet as honey in spring or bitter as the salt sea on a gray winter's morning.

At the end of *Yearwood* the boy has found answers to all the questions he knew to ask: his name, his father, and his heritage. Yet nothing is solved, for his knowledge only brings more questions, and to gain those answers he must abandon the very heritage that he has sought for so long.

The name of ROBERT A. HEINLEIN is indelibly connected with science fiction, but a very few of his works can be described as fantasy. "Magic, Inc." first appeared in that famous magazine *Unknown* and, like so many stories from that periodical, presented a world where magic is used on absolutely logical terms. Heinlein's s-f had always approached matters from an engineering rather than a pure-science viewpoint, and the magic in "Magic, Inc." was treated in the same way.

His short story, "The Man Who Traveled in Elephants" was a small, nostalgic tribute to American fairs and carnivals, curiously reminiscent of Bradbury.

And the novel *Glory Road* is a *tour de force* performance that delights lovers of both fantasy and science fiction. In this tale of a young man who answers a mysterious advertisement and finds himself on a quest that involves magic swords, beautiful princesses, and dragons, as well as many other traditionally fantastical elements, it is only near the end that the reader is given a science-fictional rationale for all this, and even the most dyed-in-the-wool Tolkien lover will have had such a good time that it doesn't matter. (b. 1907)

The Englishman WILLIAM HOPE HODGSON could well be called the Herman Melville of fantasy, since the sea plays a major role in most of his fiction; the sea, in turn, played a major role in his life. Much of the early part of it was spent as a seaman, which led to winning the Royal Humane Society's medal for heroism as well as involvement in the crusade for seamen's rights. He was also a pioneering body-builder, a lecturer, and a photographer of talent when that art was relatively new. He was killed in World War I.

Out of this curious mélange came some of the most original stories of the supernatural yet written (as well as the unique work of science fiction, *The Night Land*). Most of the short stories and two of the four novels are laid at sea. *The Ghost Pirates* concerns a sailing ship, in the days before radio, haunted by homicidal presences who are decimating the crew one by one. The claustrophobic hopelessness of the situation works brilliantly.

The Boats of the Glen Carrig begins just after a shipwreck (again in the era of sail); the two lifeboats encounter strange and weird things in the uncharted sea in which they find themselves, ending in a kind of Sargasso where are trapped the hulks of many vessels dating far back in history. The sea of weeds is infested with manlike amphibians and giant squid; here is adventure writing of the most classically thrilling variety.

The House on the Borderland is as unlike any other fantasy as *The Night Land* is unlike any other work of s-f, and is practically impossible to describe. A reclusive young man rents an old house in Ireland; the house is found to be built over a huge pit, from which emerge strange swinelike beings who lay siege to it, as the young man begins to take hallucinatory trips in time and to strange, alien landscapes. What could have been, in lesser hands, a farrago of mushily metaphysical elements is transformed by Hodgson into a terrifying, if not totally coherent, tale of the super-supernatural.

A word about *The Night Land*. This huge (*200,000 words!*) novel of a future so distant that the Earth has stopped and total night lies across it includes many of the elements of terror that Hodgson uses in his other works. The reader who prefers the dark elements of the supernatural story to the chromium brightness of science fiction will enjoy it immensely. (1877–1918)

The German E. T. A. HOFFMANN, whose short life spanned the end of the eighteenth century and the beginning of the nineteenth, was one of the writers who shaped coherent fantasy as we know it. As E. F. Bleiler notes in his introduction to *The Best Tales of Hoffmann*, he is regarded by many as the culmination of the German Romantic period.

Not for him the earlier romantic fantasies of the rural supernatural beings of the past, such as *sylphides* and sirens. Much of his magic is evoked in the cities and among the sophisticated of his own time. Science and the supernatural were closer in his day; among the fantastic elements in his fiction are mesmerism, curious psychological phenomena, and, again and again, mechanical automata (certainly the immediate ancestors of robots) who sometimes achieved a life and will of their own.

Not that the supernatural is neglected. There are

doppelgängers (unnatural duplicates of persons) and even fantasy realms visited by his contemporary characters.

It's somewhat ironic that Hoffmann's work should be best known now through operas and ballets by other people, since he himself was an accomplished composer. His first major work was the *music* for an opera, *Undine*, based on a story by his friend, de la Motte Fouqué. But now every literate person knows his written output through the opera *The Tales of Hoffmann* (based on elements from several tales) by Offenbach, and the ballets, *The Nutcracker* (based on "Nutcracker and the King of the Mice") and *Coppélia* (from the dancing doll in "The Sand-Man") by Tchaikovsky and Délibes, respectively.

Approaching Hoffmann in print rather than on the stage nowadays might be problematical for the reader; it may all seem a bit slow and wordy. Bleiler lays the blame for this square in the laps of the Victorian translators into English. But however inaccessible the tales of Hoffmann are today, their influence has been pervasive. (1776-1822)

ROBERT E. HOWARD, like his friend and colleague as writer for *Weird Tales*, H. P. Lovecraft, succeeded in establishing a contemporary mythology which has grown far beyond his own writings. Also as with Lovecraft, Howard did not live to see how popular his creations were to become; he committed suicide in 1936 at the age of thirty-one. It would certainly never have crossed his mind that he would be thought of by many as one of the two major twentieth-century influences on fantasy (the other is Tolkien, of course).

Others associate him exclusively with blood-and-thunder barbarian tales, "sword-and-sorcery" in its worst sense. This is a limited view, if not an unfair one. He certainly wrote in that vein; in a sense he created it. He wrote, in fact, in any vein, in any genre that would sell to the fiction magazines of his day—westerns, historical adventure, stories of the boxing ring, stories of the sea, science fiction, or fantasy or tales of horror. And, less commercially, he wrote a good deal of poetry.

For a decade after his death, it seemed as if his writing

would be consigned to the oblivion of flaking pulp pages and one anthology; interest in serious fantasy during and after World War II was at a low ebb. And unlike Lovecraft, he had no August Derleth to found a publishing house to perpetuate his name. But his fantasies had made their mark and a Howard cult was coalescing; in 1955 the Hyborian Legion was formed by admirers of his most popular character, the barbarian Conan and the Hyborian Age in which he lived. In the mid-'60s, when so much early science fiction and fantasy (Burroughs, Kline, Lovecraft) was rediscovered and republished, a whole new generation discovered Howard. Since then, it has seemed as if a whole new generation was *writing* Howard, as fragments were finished, series were continued, and imitations were spawned.

We are concerned here only with Howard's writings; even that is practically a lifetime study, because of his prolificacy and because so much of the output was short works, due to the magazine market he wrote for.

Besides a couple of novels in the "Conan" series, Howard's major long work is *Almuric*, which is really of that curious hybrid genre, science fantasy. The earthly hero reaches another planet by a "space-transition machine," but once there he finds it as chock full of magic and demons as any locale in Howard's fantasies.

Conan was his prime creation; around this epic character Howard wrote at least two short novels and innumerable short stories, which have been combined, recombined, sometimes retitled, and in at least one case rewritten, to the despair of bibliographers, historians, and even the readers. But in brief, Conan is a simple, unsophisticated barbarian from Cimmeria, a small backward kingdom of Earth in the Hyborian Age, a pre-ice-age period of great kingdoms, sinister sorcery, hideous demons, beautiful princesses and slave girls, and mighty battles. Given this entire world to play in and Howard's fertile imagination, Conan galumphs from one adventure to another, using brains as well as brawn to best evil (or maybe just anything that gets in the way) and gain riches, women, and power, none of which he is satisfied with for very long—then it's off to the next brouhaha.

Howard also created other memorable characters. Some readers, for instance, prefer King Kull, if only for Howard's audacious conception of his background world; it bears the same relation to the Hyborian Age as that does to ours. In other words, Kull's adventures are the legends of Conan's age, as his are of ours. (Frankly, Kull's world isn't really that different from Conan's, but is a bit more manageable. There are comparatively only a few Kull stories.)

And then there are Solomon Kane, a Puritan (of all things) adventurer of the sixteenth century; Bran Mak Morn, a chieftain of the ancient Picts; and Cormac Mac Art, an Irish sea rover of the Viking Age.

Even Howard's "historical" stories often have a touch of the occult or the supernatural in them, and it's difficult to say where fantasy leaves off and history begins. Certainly they are all cut out of the same sword-wielding, thewed and thonged cloth, but Howard's embroidery on this cloth, the wonderfully imaginative settings and characters, was something new. (There is certainly a link with the stories of Lord Dunsany, but his jeweled, elegant, ironic tales of legendary ages are about as distant from Howard's straightforward action/adventure as is possible.) And with it he has captured the imaginations of tens of thousands of readers, perhaps millions with the Conan movie. (1906–1936)

In her first two fantasy novels DAHLOV IPCAR gives the reader the impression of a jazz pianist who improvises variations on familiar melodies. She combines, in *The Queen of Spells*, a haunting and simple retelling of the Scots ballad "Tam Linn," the standard elements of changelings, a Faerie Queen, love and jealousy, with her own imaginative touches. The story ranges across a span of time but most of the action takes place in nineteenth-century America, where she skillfully demonstrates the magical possibilities of the traveling circuses of that era. An actual chess match, played by two international grandmasters in 1947, provides the structure for *The Warlock of Night*, Ipcar the magic. She convincingly creates a world divided into a

78

Land of Day and a Kingdom of Night; the protagonist is the apprentice to the Warlock of Night and it is mostly through his eyes that an epic battle between the two countries is witnessed. It makes an intriguing story even for those readers whose knowledge of chess is nil.

It is in her third book, *Dark Horn Blowing*, that she makes her own melody out of various elements of European folklore. A young woman is stolen from her husband and child by the fairy folk, with the connivance of a witch who was her rival in love. She is to be nursemaid to the infant son of the hideous Elf King, who, since he can shapeshift at will, simply chooses to be hideous. In the telling of how she fares in captivity and what happens to her family when her husband is left to the seductions of the witch, Ipcar neatly shifts the reader between our world and the enchantment of Faerie. (b. 1917)

ERIC IVERSON, in his sequential novels *Wereblood* (1979) and *Werenight*, has created a fascinating land and interesting persons and things to people it. Gerin, called the Fox, is leader of a village that is one of many in his area, all of which are in peril from the Trokmo, vicious barbarians led by the evil sorcerer King Balamung. The novels detail the quest of Gerin, along with his giant friend Van and the beautiful (as well as intelligent and competent) Elise, for the aid of another sorcerer powerful enough to defeat Balamung. The land through which they travel is one of the major hazards, filled as it is with night-stalking, bloodsucking ghosts, werebeasts, and nasty mortals, and the gallants provide enough action for any but the bloodiest tastes.

JOHN JAKES, today best known for his multivolume "Kent Family Chronicles," learned his craft writing a remarkable number of novels and short stories in a variety of genres within a twenty-year period beginning in the early 1950s. Just how many is almost impossible to determine, since Jakes wrote a large portion pseudonymously.

This experience turned Jakes into a seasoned storyteller with an almost instinctive sense of pacing and a narrative style several cuts above the masters of the pulp period. In fantasy he is noted for his "Brak the Barbarian" sword-and-sorcery series (*Brak the Barbarian, Brak the Barbarian Versus the Sorceress, Brak the Barbarian Versus the Mark of the Demon*). The Brak stories have a lighter, more playful touch than Robert E. Howard's Conan tales, which they otherwise faithfully imitate. Shortly before leaving s-f and fantasy for more profitable enterprises in the mid-seventies, Jakes wrote *Mention My Name in Atlantis*, a deft and amusing parody of the clichés of sword-and-sorcery, sprinkled with a number of s-f "in" jokes. (b. 1932)

The claim can be made that one cannot be a ghost-story aficionado without knowing the work of M. R. JAMES. In fact, when one says "ghost story," the concept itself refers more accurately to James's work than any others that come to mind. "Story" implies shortness of length; James's works are marvels of succinctness. "Ghost," without getting into metaphysics, implies a malevolent manifestation of past evil attached to a particular locale or artifact. In James, these are usually aroused by some innocent (often one interested in antiquarianism, as was James himself) with horrible results.

The horror, however, is never blood and gore, and even rarely death. It comes from the more subtle implication of the breakdown in natural and moral law, enhanced by being set in the most mundane of surroundings. (James's backgrounds of Edwardian England may be a bit strange to us but hardly exotic.) It is the horror of putting your hand on something hairy, nasty, and living (more or less) in your own dark living room—when you don't own a pet.

The sense of reality is also heightened by the absolute authenticity of detail (a result of James's antiquarian interests). Lovecraft can speak of "tortured gables," but James speaks of ogival hoods, crockets, and finials.

It only needs to *précis* one James story to convey the quality on which he wove endless variation. An English scholar takes an off-season vacation by the shore. He finds an ancient Roman whistle on which is written, in Latin, "Who is this that is coming?" (The title of the story is "Oh,

Whistle, and I'll Come to You, My Lad.") He blows the whistle. Several times later, he seems to see an indistinct figure down the deserted beach; it seems to be coming nearer. And then at night something begins to stir in the extra bed in his hotel room. . . .

In this day of weighty and ororverbose "horror novels," M. R. James's short, perfect ghost stories are the exquisite Persian miniatures of the field.

(One word of warning for those who may not have read these wonderful stories. They are not to be devoured all at once. This is a bedside book, to be taken one or two stories at a time. Most of them were written for an annual event, a reading by James on Christmas Eve for his friends—by the light of a single candle.) (1862–1936)

TOVE JANSSON is a member of the Swedish-speaking minority of Finland, where she lives on an island. To judge by her Moomin books, she is obviously quite mad in the best possible way; they are probably the most original works for children to be published since the Pooh books, and possibly since *Alice*, to which they can be compared, but in no coherent way. The series, which has extended itself over the past quarter-century, achieved great popularity in Britain, where a comic strip was based on it, but, despite sporadic publication in the U.S., has never quite caught on there.

The Moomin books are among those rare works that are indescribable except in their own terms. Words such as "whimsical" and "surrealistic" come to mind (as well as just plain "mad"), but they all have the wrong connotation; most books that are whimsically surrealist are also awful, particularly for the fantasy fan who needs consistency. Consistency the Moomin books have; it's just based on some other form of logic.

Perhaps a description of the first book in the series, *Finn Family Moomintroll*, might give some of the flavor. The Moomins live in a valley by the sea. They are descended from the trolls that lived behind the stoves in Scandinavian kitchens. Moomin is more or less the hero. Moominmomma is the epitomal mother, despite an overexcessive attachment to her handbag. Moominpappa tends to go on at length about the adventures of his youth (a later book in the series is his memoirs). Living with the Moomin family is a motley assortment of characters. The Snork and his sister, the Snork Maiden, seem to be variant Moomins. Snufkin is an independent type in a crushed hat who hates belongings and Park Keepers and staying in one place. Sniff is a young sort of creature who is insecure and reminiscent of Piglet. There is the Hemulin, who wears a dress he inherited from his aunt and always curtsies ("because it looks silly to bow in a dress"). He is also literal-minded, unhappy when not collecting something, and a nit-picker.

There is a misanthropic muskrat who is writing a book on *The Uselessness of Everything*; the Hattifatteners, a mysterious race who can neither hear nor speak, and spend their lives in migration except for the yearly gathering on an island to worship a barometer; the Groke, who sits and stares and freezes the ground beneath her; and a whole cast of small creatures who live their own lives underfoot.

The plot of this particular volume is a classic situation, the finding of a magic artifact and the mischief that results. Moomin and company come upon the Hobgoblin's hat and use it for a wastepaper basket; little do they realize that anything placed in it is subject to mysterious changes. The climax comes when Moominmomma drops a clump of poisonous pink perennials (part of the Hemulin's botanical collection) into the hat and the Moominhouse becomes a jungle, in which the characters play Tarzan and Jane. ("Moomintroll produced a Tarzan roar from the top of the airing cupboard, and Jane and the rest of them roared back.") And then the Hobgoblin comes for his hat....

Try it. *You* may just be mad enough to like it.

DIANA WYNNE JONES doesn't write like Diana Wynne Jones; the only stylistic similarity among her novels is the high quality of the writing and the imagination in plotting and characterization. Her work spans a range from juveniles which will be enjoyed by any aficionado of children's literature (*The Ogre Downstairs* and *Witch's Business*, a.k.a. *Wilkin's Tooth*) to a strange and wonderful series set in the imaginary land of Dalemark.

Between these two extremes falls most of her other work. There is *Eight Days of Luke*, an excellent usage of Norse mythology in a present-day setting, which also includes a very clever and fitting depiction of Valhalla; there is *Charmed Life*, a story set in a world where magic is a relatively common occurrence. Gwendolyn and her brother, Cat, orphans, are invited to stay at the castle of Chrestomanci, supreme magician of the land. Gwendolyn's a witch, while Cat thinks he's a nothing, and the thrust of the story is the discovery by both of who and what they really are. *The Magicians of Caprona* is a sequel, in that it's set in the same world, but is a little different—a sort of magical and not so tragic telling of *Romeo and Juliet*.

The magic and writing of *The Power of Three* and *Dogsbody* is more intense than of the books mentioned above. The first is a fascinating tale concerning the conflict among the three species that live on the Moor—the Mound People, the Dorig, and the Giants. It falls to three children of the respective species to attempt to lift an ancient curse laid on the Moor by a Dorig murdered for its golden collar. *Dogsbody* opens with the trial of Sirius, the dog star, by the other luminaries for the murder of another star and the loss of an object of power. Sirius is sentenced to Earth in the body of a dog, and must find the object within the life span of the dog or die. The story is told from the dog's point of view, and among other things (such as awesome magic from Earth, Sun, and Moon) contains a thrilling and chilling representation of the Wild Hunt.

The "Dalemark Sequence," projected for five novels and named for the land in which it takes place, is not a series in the accepted sense. Two of the books, *Cart and Cwidder* and *Drowned Ammet*, start in the same town and time but go in entirely different directions, the former being the story of a band of traveling musicians thrown into the political turmoil that is overtaking the land, while *Ammet* deals with the older gods and customs of Dalemark. There is magic in the land, but it is with a quiet power that it happens. A third novel, *The Spellcoats*, set in prehistoric Dalemark, is probably best read last, so that the reader has a "now" on which to base the people and magic of the "then." A truly wonderful work, it is the story of a young girl weaving a story into a coat in such a way that it affects the story she is weaving. The first coat may be a bit confusing, but when the second is woven the tale becomes clear and ends with one of the most powerful pieces of magic in the fantasy realm. (b. 1934)

Much "children's" fantasy is disliked by adults because there seems to be too much emphasis on learning and growth and other meaningful things, but CAROL KENDALL, in her Minnipin duet, has the meaningful things happen to such likable characters that the meaning doesn't get in the way of the enjoyment. *The Gammage Cup* is a delightful novel about a few minnipins (small beings who act and look much like humans) who don't want to act exactly like the other minnipins and are exiled for their eccentricities, but then save their village and all the other minnipins from an ancient and terrible enemy. The major characters are the slightly scatterbrained Muggles, bard and adventurer Gummy, Walter the Earl, historian, and miserly Mingy. They and others in the exiled group make for a fun company in travail. *The Whisper of Glocken* is a sequel, stressing endurance and courage rather than noncomformity. (b. 1917)

STEPHEN KING is the premier horror writer of our time; he is one of the few modern writers who really deserve to hit the best-seller lists with every book, and for a simple reason. He is a craftsman. His plots, although sometimes simple, always hang together. His characters are more than just believable, they are *real*. And his pacing—oh, God, his pacing. Some people don't scare easily; at his best Stephen King can leave even them quivering in broad daylight. It is the pacing and the vivid descriptive style that mark King as more than just good. He has the ability to maintain a pitch of terror, to stretch it over a longer time than anyone who hasn't read his books would believe possible. The main body of *The Shining* is 441 pages long, and it *never* lets up.

It is somewhat pointless to describe the plots of King's novels; no synopsis can convey the *frisson* of terror that even the memory of the books can bring. Briefly, then, there's *Carrie*, the frightened and frightening girl that you all made fun of when you were in high school. *Salem's Lot* is a small New England town with a vampire on the loose. In *The Shining* (which King wanted to call simply *Shine*), the walls have memories, and memories have power (please, dear reader, don't confuse the book with the movie —when the film was done, little remained of the novel). *The Stand* is about the end of the world; *The Dead Zone* is about the end of a man. *Firestarter* is a pyrotechnic work about what happens when the government really wants something you have. "The Mist" (found in the anthology *Dark Forces*, edited by Kirby McCauley) is a story about creepy, crawly, HORRIBLE things, and may well be the scariest work of fiction ever written.

There is some dispute, in circles where they dispute such things, as to whether King is really a fantasist or an s-f writer. Unquestionably many of his horrors come from a laboratory, and there is a case to be made for psychic abilities as science. But fantasy is what takes place behind the eyes, and that is where fear lives. Whether the fear is engendered by a vampire or by deadly microbes is irrelevant; the point is to dredge up those deep unreasoning fears that live in the bottom ooze of the human mind. That is Stephen King's skill, and that is why he is fantasist, showing us the darker side of the genre. (b. 1946)

It isn't often noted that RUDYARD KIPLING, that epitomal "imperialist," probably did more than any other European to translate the wonder and beauty that is India into terms understandable to his countrymen in the nineteenth century. Two of the major works by which this was accomplished were *The Jungle Book* and *The Second Jungle Book*, which also centered on one of the primal fantasies of all time, the human child raised by animals. The boy Mowgli, fostered by wolves, taught by a bear, a leopard, and a python, implacable enemy of the tiger, Shere Khan, lives one of the great adventure stories, set in the exotic beauty of the Indian jungles, swarming with wildlife and teeming with vegetation hiding lost cities of stone.

Anyone who has avoided the Jungle Books because they are "classics"—or worse, for fear of cutely Disneyesque talking animals—should remedy the situation immediately. Kipling's sharply drawn animal characters are far from cute (though sometimes lovable), and they live in a world where death is always present. The stories about Mowgli are interspersed with others about the domestic animals of the Anglo-Indian army, the valiant mongoose, Rikki-Tikki-Tavi, and, in an abrupt change of scene, a seal of the far northern ocean.

Kipling's other major fantasy is far less well known. *Puck of Pook's Hill* is that very Puck from *A Midsummer Night's Dream*, and he takes two English children into the past with him to meet various inhabitants of the British Isles of different periods, all of whom have fascinating stories to tell of their own eras. Though without the power and poetry of the Jungle Books, a jollier way to learn English history has never been devised. It, too, has a sequel, *Rewards and Fairies*.

There are also some fascinating and little-known short stories, such as " 'They,'" " 'Wireless,'" and "The Finest Story in the World." In short, as the old joke[1] would have it, if you've never Kippled, you should. (1865–1936)

RICHARD KIRK has created a sword-and-sorcery epic that outclasses almost all the competition. *Raven, Swordsmistress of Chaos*, heroine of the series that bears her name, is a young, fearfully abused slave girl. She is chosen by Fate, or possibly by the mysterious sorcerers of the Ghost Isle of Kharwhan, to be the focus on Earth for the forces of Chaos—to be the instrument of Chaos in the destruction of order, law, civilization, all the things that men hold dear. This is an Elder Earth, before the Fall, and from the very beginning we know that Chaos has triumphed—

---

[1] "Do you like Kipling?" "I don't know. I've never Kippled."

we just don't know quite how. So we follow Raven being led by her destiny through hatred and murder, love and betrayal, through a landscape of glittering kingdoms and loathsome realms. We watch her transformation from helpless slave to mistress of all weapons, and from victim to nemesis.

These books (there are five) have a little of everything: sex and violence, deadly sorcerers, dashing swordsmen, horrible dangers, pirates, gods and demons, and a glorious heroine. Kirk has created a rich, coherent world with some surprising philosophical twists. Perhaps most surprising of all, the "Raven" series is very well written—if you have never really liked sword-and-sorcery, give Raven a try. If you are already a fan of the subgenre, you will be delighted.

KATHERINE KURTZ has produced a long series (six books so far) set in an alternate-world Wales, where a portion of the population have magical abilities. These people, the Deryni, quite naturally became the rulers of normal men and women by force of their power; but the rising tide of Christianity, coupled with revulsion for the excesses of the Deryni king and nobility, brought about a popular revolution, led by those few Deryni lords who cared for their human subjects. Inevitably, after the successful rebellion, the common folk and human lords forgot that some Deryni were their friends, and remembered only the evils of tyranny. As generations passed, it became more and more dangerous to be Deryni, until, as the first book, *Deryni Rising*, opens, to be known as Deryni or even suspected is to be declared a heretic and traitor. The only exception to this rule is Lord Alaric Morgan, Duke of Corwyn, the half-Deryni friend of the King. In this and the following two books (*Deryni Checkmate* and *High Deryni*) Morgan and the young King Kelson struggle to secure the kingdom of Gwynedd against the onslaught of a full-Deryni claimant to the throne.

Camber of Culdi, *Saint Camber*, and *Camber the Heretic* tell the story of the Deryni Lord Camber, who was the leader of the revolt that deposed the Deryni dynasty. Although chronologically the action occurs many decades before *Deryni Rising*, these books were written some years after, and many concepts are more fully explained in Kurtz's first books. Reading in the order written makes for a richer experience. (b. 1944)

The inclusion of HENRY KUTTNER in a volume on fantasy may draw some argument from those who think of him solely as a science-fiction writer, but that argument would almost have to come down to the last few chapters of many of his novels, and the matter of style would also come in for some discussion. Much of his work may be called "rationalized" fantasy, in that the way it is written and the events that occur are in every way good fantasy, but it ends with a scientific or pseudoscientific explanation. *The Dark World*, for example, is a marvelous sword-and-sorcery novel, with intelligent animals (wolves, horses, and eagles) contending along with humanity against a lost race. Only in the end does one receive the rationale. *The Mask of Circe* is another wonderful work, in which a descendant of Jason (of Golden Fleece fame) is thrown into a world of classical mythology. In this one the gods are real, but their powers just don't happen to be supernatural.

And for those who are not convinced by the novels, there are Kuttner's short stories: "A Gnome There Was," in which a mortal strays into the wrong tunnel in a mine and ends up in the hall of a mountain king who is at least as slovenly and cantankerous as Ibsen's and with none of the grandeur Grieg gave him; or "The Graveyard Rats," a masterful excursion into sheer terror; or there are the stories about Elak of Atlantis, a sort of Conanesque character in Lovecraftian settings.

So argue if you will about Henry Kuttner, but if you read his work there will be joy in your preparation for debate. (1915–1958)

R. A. LAFFERTY doesn't see the world in quite the same way that most people do; his logic is rigorous, but his premises are deadpan insanity. His fantasies often take the form of "tall tales"—one is not expected to believe them literally but should at least have the courtesy to listen, and approve if the tale is well told.

"The Devil Is Dead" trilogy, of which only two volumes have been published, is about the wanderings of Finnegan (everybody knows Finnegan!) and his meddling into the secrets of the Devil. The books range time and space, and sail all the seas, especially the lost ones, punctuated by almost-comprehensible verse and almost-meaningful aphorisms. The three books are called *Archipelago*, *The Devil Is Dead*, and *More Than Melchisedech*.

Lafferty's short stories also range far and wide, from tales of people who live in river mud to psychedelic kaleidoscopic cobras that run amok among the asteroids. He tells about prophets and seers and lonely computers, the suicide pacts of children, and seashells that can tell you everything. He is hard to classify (most genius is); we call him a fantasist since that comes closest and the world doesn't like people who don't wear labels. R. A. Lafferty writes lafferties. Sometimes Thorne Smith wrote lafferties, too, but Smith's lack the pungent, intoxicating wildness of the real thing. (b. 1914)

SANDERS ANNE LAUBENTHAL has produced in *Excalibur* what seems at first to be a paradox, an Arthurian fantasy set in present-day Mobile, Alabama. But, combining the legendary voyage of Welsh Prince Mardoc to America in 1170 with the assumption that he may have carried on board Arthur's sword Excalibur, she weaves a plausible fantasy and a poignant love story. The discovery of the site of the Welsh colony by the current Pendragon brings him into conflict with the ageless Morgan le Fay and the evil force that her sister Morgeuse has become. Ms. Laubenthal is an adept writer and the age-old conflict between Light and Dark is handled with a modern complexity of plot and characterization. (b. 1943)

ROBERT LAWSON was both author and illustrator. His distinctive pen-and-ink drawings graced such modern children's classics as *Mr. Popper's Penguins* and the Homer Price stories. Lawson was also a warm and witty humorist, with a keen love of animals that permeates all his books for young people.

Rabbit Hill, his best-known work, concerns the apprehensions of a clan of rabbits, and other assorted woodland creatures, about the new inhabitants of a derelict farmhouse. Its naïve optimism and sentimentality may be a bit strong for some, but the story is heartwarming in the most sincere sense. *Ben and Me* is the tale of a poor churchmouse named Amos who finds a home in Ben Franklin's bonnet and secretly guides his career. *Mr. Revere and I,* a slightly more adult variation on the theme, concerns a haughty mare who escapes from her cruel British master and comes to play a crucial role in the birth of the American Republic. Lawson's unflattering illustrations of gaunt, seedy, scruffy revolutionaries and portly redcoats contribute an added immediacy to both books. (b. 1892)

While many writers of fantasy deal in existing mythology or legend, TANITH LEE's forte is in creating her own. *Night's Master* and *Death's Master,* two closely related books, contain the legends about two demons, Azhrarn and Uhlume, and their dealings with the men and women of Earth. Lee's demonkind are a masterful creation, so convincingly nonhuman that their occasional lapses into human impulses and motives seem fully as bizarre to the reader as to the other demons. The form of the story is similar to existing mythology—each episode is a complete tale in itself, with its own point to make, but the threads of many longer sagas can be followed in and out of the work, parting and coming together to make a delicately textured whole.

Kill the Dead is in essence a ghost story, the spare recounting of the confrontation of a "ghost-killer" with the meaning of his own life. For this book Lee has abandoned the exuberant descriptive style that marks her other work in favor of a brooding, shadowy tone that is complementary to the ascetic, driven nature of the hero.

Lee's first book, *The Birthgrave,* and its two sequels, *Vazkor, Son of Vazkor* and *Quest for the White Witch,* create an interesting problem for fantasy purists. In style, form, and subject matter they are strictly sword-and-sorcery. In *The Birthgrave*, a woman with magical powers awakens in the heart of a volcano without memory of her history, her race, or her name. Leaving the flaming mountain, she enters the world of mortal men, where she is believed to be and perhaps is a goddess. Magical adventure, terrible wars, and sorcerous enemies follow her over the face of the world, until in the end she is reunited with her son and is able to gather together others who have some of the abilities of her race. The problem of classification (whether the books are fantasy or science fiction) is posed at the end of *The Birthgrave*. Here the nameless heroine encounters a spaceship and with the aid of the ship's computer recovers her identity and her past. The star voyagers are from the planet Earth, and have been surveying this world for many generations, watching its history unfold. Yet despite the *deus ex machina* and the s-f categorization, the series appeals strongly to the fantasy audience. (b. 1947)

Given the many trumpery spinners of tales of the supernatural in the nineteenth century, SHERIDAN LE FANU stands alone for his intelligence and style. (Sheridan, really his middle name, indicates a kinship with Richard Brinsley Sheridan, the dramatist.) A journalist and something of a recluse in his later life, Le Fanu wrote not only of supernatural happenings but of the psychological reactions and involvements of the people affected by them.

For instance, in what may be his best known work, the novelette *Carmilla*, the beautiful and immortal vampire, Carmilla, not only wishes the blood of the heroine, but approaches her on emotional levels, also, to the extent of giving the story strongly erotic lesbian overtones. It preceded Stoker's *Dracula* by twenty years or so and still makes excellent reading, particularly strong on atmosphere. Inevitably with such elements, *Carmilla* has attracted film makers and there have been several movies based on it, notably the three that make up the "Karnstein trilogy," horror films of more than average interest. (There is also a sort of inside joke in the fine version of *Dracula* made for the BBC, in which the Count speaks lovingly of the Karnstein sisters; Karnstein is Carmilla's ancestral home.)

Le Fanu's other short works are of equal quality, and the novel *Uncle Silas* has been compared favorably to *The Woman in White* and *The Moonstone* as an atmospheric mystery. (1814–1873)

In a world where all too few people see the fantasy inherent in reality (or the reality inherent in fantasy, for that matter), URSULA K. LE GUIN is exercising her not inconsiderable abilities to demonstrate just that. Le Guin's most serious works of fantasy are *Orsinian Tales* and *Malafrena*, set in a world not very different from our own, just as hard, real, one might almost say mundane, as our own. *Orsinian Tales* is a collection of folk tales from the land of Orsinia; *Malafrena* is a novel, set in Orsinia, about a young student. Orsinia is a middle-European country with its own history, very much a part of the real world. In these works, the fantasy is not so much within the tales, but in their very existence—they invite the reader to become the fantasist, to cast disbelief to the winds and accept that Orsinia exists, and revel in some of its finest literature.

Le Guin's earlier fantasy, the "Earthsea Trilogy," is something else again. Here are no games of perception, no pushing at the boundaries of Faerie. Earthsea is set in an overtly magical world, complete with wizards, demons, and enchantments. The tale concerns a young boy named Ged and his education as a wizard; an education which forces him to face the darker side of his own soul. Although written with the young in mind, the "Earthsea Trilogy" (*A Wizard of Earthsea*, *The Tombs of Atuan*, and *The Farthest Shore*) is an exciting, magical adventure for all ages.

Yet another aspect of Ursula Le Guin's role in fantasy can be found in her numerous essays on the subject, collected in *Languages of the Night*. Here she probes into the nature of fantasy in literature and reveals much of the careful reasoning behind her own particular style of fantasy. (b. 1929)

If some sort of impossible equation could be extracted from number of works written plus variety of works written plus quality of works written, FRITZ LEIBER might well come up with the highest score across the various subgenres of fantasy. This topnotch writer has been going since the days of the great *Unknown* magazine; he is a multiple award winner for his science fiction, is equally well known for his chilling supernatural works, and in the realm of pure fantasy he managed to be well into a series of stories that were delightful and rollicking satires of sword-and-sorcery before that subgenre had enough entries to be called sword-and-sorcery.

Perhaps typical of this protean talent's many-faceted stories is the classic *Conjure Wife*. It is set amid the groves of academe, back in the days when colleges and universities were ivory towers of peace and quiet. This renders all the more shocking its portrayal of the faculty wives using malevolent witchcraft to further their husbands' careers, and not stopping short of torture and death for those who get in the way.

Aha! you say, it is a novel of the supernatural. But the magic used is presented to be as much of an exact science as that taught by the professors, which has led many to consider it a work of science fiction, merely concerning a science about which not much is known. No simple pigeonholing here, but simply a superb story.

The aforementioned satirical series consists of the stories about Fafhrd and the Gray Mouser; they are even liked by those who hate sword-and-sorcery. The stories take place on the world called Nehwon, which many of the inhabitants believe to be on the *inside* of a bubble which is rising through infinite waters. Fafhrd is a barbarian from the North with as many muscles and appetites as Conan, but a good deal less sense. This is supplied by the Gray Mouser, who is short on massive musculature, but very long on foxiness.

These two companions, more or less boon and more or less constant (they're not above crossing each other up at times), steal, lie, cheat, shoplift, and connive their way across the exotic world of Nehwon, involved in a thousand and one adventures contrived by Leiber's fertile imagination. There are sorcerers good and bad, there are female ghouls with transparent flesh, there are princesses who are wererats, there are travelers in crosstime machines who speak German and are collecting animals for a "Time Zoo"; in short, there are infinite wonders to be explored with the pair.

There are, in fact, infinite wonders to be explored with Fritz Leiber. To go out on a limb, the statement might be made (and few authors can it be made of) that you can't go wrong with any of his many short stories, collected in numerous anthologies, or his too-infrequent novels. (b. 1910)

C. S. LEWIS, that formidable Anglican theologian, wrote in his autobiography that he became a Christian when he was "surprised by Joy." As a fantasist he returned the gift to his readers by infusing his books with childlike wonder and that deep, bubbling wellspring of delight that is Joy. Lewis was a part of the influential but informal Oxford literary group, the Inklings; the membership also included Tolkien and Charles Williams. They were friends and mutual critics, whose weekly gathering always ended with readings by each from their works in progress. Mystic Christians all, these men shared a vision of the world derived in large part from the writings of George MacDonald; his beliefs about good and evil, his mystical vision of the Deity and the world, are the fundamentals behind Tolkien's *Silmarillion* and Lewis's Narnia books.

"The Chronicles of Narnia" is a seven-book series about a world a little to one side of our own; it is the country of belief, entered unexpectedly by the childlike, and always beyond the reach of the "grown-up." The first in the series, *The Lion, the Witch, and the Wardrobe,* is about four children, Peter, Susan, Edmund, and Lucy, who stumble into Narnia through the back of an old wardrobe. They discover that they are destined to save the land from the rule of an evil witch. In the second, *Prince Caspian,* the four return to Narnia thousands of years after they left it to restore a young king to his throne. Third is *The Voyage of the Dawn Treader*; Edmund and Lucy go on a voyage of discovery with King Caspian, taking along their reprehensible cousin

Eustace. In *The Silver Chair*, the reformed Eustace and a friend go to the rescue of a captive prince. *The Horse and His Boy* takes place during the reign of High King Peter, and tells of a Narnian Horse and a lost prince who make their way back to Narnia.

Throughout these five books, Narnia and all in it are guarded, guided, inspired and redeemed by Aslan, the Lord of the world, a Christ figure who takes the form of a giant, wildly beautiful golden Lion. The sixth book, *The Magician's Nephew*, tells how humans first entered Narnia and contains a powerful, *joyful* description of Aslan creating the world: the golden Lion, pacing slowly over the barren landscape, singing. As he sings, all living things spring up in his tracks. The final book, *The Last Battle*, is the story of the end of Narnia, its dismantling by Aslan after the reason for its existence is done.

A more important book, although less well known, is *Till We Have Faces*. This is a complex, intricate novel, subject to many interpretations. The basic story is a retelling of the myth of Cupid and Psyche, but here the teller is Psyche's oldest sister, and the tale is not a simple story of the gods and men, but an encounter between a rational woman and a living god's demand for faith. Oraul, the oldest daughter of the king of Glome, is as ugly as her little sister Psyche is beautiful, but Psyche loves her. When Psyche is chosen by the priests to be a sacrifice to the angry Goddess of Glome and Psyche is willing to die for the people, Oraul conceives a hatred for the gods and herself that remains for the rest of her life. *Till We Have Faces* is both realistic and mythic; it chronicles the day-to-day life of an isolated kingdom in Hellenic times, while incorporating the mystical presence of the gods in that life. The book is a parable on the nature of Faith, one of Lewis's abiding concerns, and is written in his most luminous and engaging style. (1898–1963)

DAVID LINDSAY was a poor writer, with an awkward prose style, but one who had an overpowering concept of reality that he was driven to try to communicate. As a writer he was groping toward a description of the higher states of being, a true geometry of the soul, but he was confined by convention to the novel, a medium that, except in the hands of a master, is not well suited to the precise statement of metaphysical insights.

Lindsay's most famous book is *A Voyage to Arcturus*, a metaphysical s-f allegory; it is by far the most successful of his books and the most clearly written. His other novels are fantasies, books strangly reminiscent of Charles Williams but lacking Williams's deft touch. The most accessible is *The Violet Apple*, where a man and a woman, each engaged to another, are brought to the realization that they are perfect mates. The means to this knowledge are two tiny apples from an ancient, mystical tree.

The Haunted Woman is considered by many of Lindsay's devotees to be his most compelling work. In it, a phantom staircase leads to a house's nonexistent upper storey. In this place a man and woman meet and fall in love. This is a tragedy, for when the lovers return to the lower parts of the house they cannot remember anything that has happened in the upper storey.

Two other books of Lindsay's have been published: *The Witch*, which was never finished but is still vintage Lindsay, and *Sphinx*, a book which is hard to locate these days. There is yet a sixth novel by Lindsay, although it has never been published. The book is called *Devil's Tor*, and by repute it is longer and more convoluted than *A Voyage to Arcturus*. The theme is apparently the return to Earth of the Great Mother Goddess, and the coming of a new aeon.

While David Lindsay's style is not to everyone's taste, he is not a writer to be lightly dismissed. His thoughts were profound and his influence is growing steadily. (1878–1945)

HUGH LOFTING wrote a series of twelve books about the most famous veterinarian in the world, John Doolittle, M.D. Doctor Doolittle, of course, began his career in medicine as a physician to human beings; it was his love of animals and the tutelage of his parrot, Polynesia, that made him turn, late in life, to the medical treatment of animals. Because, you see, what Polynesia taught him was how to speak to animals in their own languages. After that Doctor Doolittle's life became rather peculiar.

Lofting's books are wonderful and absurd, and Doolittle's charm is that he is so much more innocent and impractical than his animal friends. He is the image of the British country doctor—short, fat, and graying, with his medical bag under his arm—but there all resemblance ends. Dr. Doolittle can't quite get the hang of money, he finds it amusing to be thrown into jail, and he can't see any reason on Earth why he shouldn't set off on a journey to Africa (or elsewhere) at a moment's notice. And he does, frequently; Doolittle's travels take him to the aid of animals everywhere on Earth.

The books have a deadly-earnest silliness about them, which is probably what has made them the favorites of generations of children. Lofting never underestimated his readers; he might explain things occasionally, but he never talked down. Doolittle himself, while a Very Important Man, is essentially a child. He delights in dangerous adventure, he performs feats of courage and nobility, and, most important, he always wins in the end. Yet the doctor also knows the pleasure of playing in mudpuddles, and spends hours watching a bug or plunging his head underwater to learn the language of a fish.

In recent years some criticism has been made of the Doolittle books because of their racial stereotypes, but, considering that the stories were written between 1914 and 1930, Lofting did a fairly good job of evenhandedly lampooning all humanity regardless of race. The biases of the books are the biases of children, who would prefer their Red Indians to be skulking in the underbrush, their Africans to be cannibals, and their recluses to be hiding from a wrongful accusation of murder.

The Doctor Doolittle books are a delight, from the housekeeping duck to the giant glass-shelled sea snail; no lover of the ridiculous should dismiss them as purely children's fare. (1886–1947)

The career of FRANK BELKNAP LONG is one of astonishing longevity as well as astonishing variety. His first published story appeared in 1924, and he has contributed a new story to the 1980 *New Tales of the Cthulhu Mythos.*

The latter publication is ironic in a way; Long was reportedly the first author permitted by Lovecraft to use his Cthulhu mythos, and it is rather wonderful to find him contributing a "new tale" along with such relatively young authors as Stephen King and Ramsey Campbell.

Long is often thought of, in fact, as a somewhat lesser Lovecraft; this is a limited and rather unfair view. His work is much more varied, much less confined to that one note that Lovecraft seemed to strike over and over. Almost all of his longer works, in fact, have been highly creditable science fiction that is a good deal closer to that genre as we know it than Lovecraft's oblique "science fantasy."

Those shorter works that *are* in the horror-fantasy vein will certainly be enjoyed by Lovecraft fans, but even those who find Lovecraft's extravagant prose hard to take might well like Long's slightly more humorous, definitely more humanistic approach.

Long has also done an affectionate and informative biography of Lovecraft. (b. 1903)

It seems that H. P. LOVECRAFT is here to stay—his work, that is, and his influence. There could have been some doubt thirty years ago, when he was a virtually unknown writer whom his friends and colleagues were promoting after an early and rather sad demise, and there could have been some doubt a decade ago when he was suddenly a well-known writer with a rock group named after him. (It takes some sort of potential immortality to survive that.)

But this lonely, lantern-jawed New Englander who wanted nothing more than to be an eighteenth-century gentleman, and who made a living rewriting and typing the manuscripts of writers far less talented than he for pathetic pennies per word, has caught the imagination of several succeeding generations now, and that's enough, it seems, for his reputation to endure.

Though often called "the successor to Poe" and identified in the public mind as primarily a writer of the supernatural, Lovecraft emerged from that period of magazine fantasy when the supernatural and science fiction were much closer (a ghost or a Martian were equally likely to

most of the readers in that unscientifically trained age).
Much of his work can be called science fiction, since he often gave pseudoscientific rationales for the terrifying creatures he visited on humanity from the "gulfs beyond." In
reality, his stories lie astraddle the territory between high-
tech and horror.

Lovecraft certainly meant to horrify, of course, but he
would have been horrified himself at today's explicit violence and gore. While subtlety, perhaps, is not the word for
his approach, it is by innuendo and concept rather than inspired revulsion that we are terrified, that we come to feel
the universe is not so subject to sane, "natural" laws as we
may think.

As a matter of fact, there is a subtler level to Lovecraft's
writings not often cited but still adding much to the general unease that his stories evoke. Aside from his repul-
sive, tentacled, "squamous" (there's a good Lovecraftian
word), and lethal beings, his humans are often just as re-
pugnant in a less spectacular mode, often described as
inbred and decayed (in a genealogical sense, but sometimes
also literally). This view of a subnormal strain of humanity
is certainly out of fashion in this egalitarian day and age,
but it still rings true.

A prime example is his description of the inhabitants of
Innsmouth, his other fictional Massachusetts town (Arkham is the best known), in *The Shadow over Innsmouth*
(sometimes known as *The Weird Shadow over Innsmouth*),
one of his longer works that tends to the other side of the
spectrum from the science-fictional. A traveler is forced to
spend the night in this unpleasant, decaying port, and the
horror is manifested not in any terrible thingie but in the
claustrophobic oppressiveness of being in an alien place
where malevolent forces are gathering unheard and un-
seen. The reader soon wants to get out of the loathsome locale as much as the protagonist does.

His other longer work that tends more to the horrific
end of the scale is *The Case of Charles Dexter Ward*, which
is in a sense epitomal of this area of Lovecraft's writing.
The hero begins to research his ancestors, in particular one
who lived in eighteenth-century colonial Massachusetts.
He finds more than he bargained for, and revives the un-

speakable horrors which that ancestor had brought up in his time.

Over both these works and most others of Lovecraft's hovers the shadow of the Cthulhu mythos, that pantheon of dread and demonic deities that once owned Earth and intend to do so again. Half theology, half s-f, it is an amazing and original framework which is revealed piecemeal so convincingly that many readers are taken in to believe in its reality. (Booksellers are used to being asked for the fictional *Necronomicon*, a "forbidden" book that is one of the cornerstones of knowledge of the mythos. Other books have since used that title, but Lovecraft's *Necronomicon*— or more correctly, Abdul Alhazrad's—does not exist. And just as well.)

Lovecraft's longest work, and perhaps the most atypical, comes from relatively early in his writing career, when he was much under the influence of Lord Dunsany. It is called *The Dream Quest of Unknown Kadath* and the title tells it; it is indeed a phantasmagorical dream journey, very nineteenth-century in its resemblance to George MacDonald's *Phantastes* and even Lewis Carroll's Alice books. The Dunsanian influence is certainly there in the lush Oriental imagery, but there is also reference to the Cthulhu mythology. All in all, it's an odd mélange but an interesting one, and well worth reading.

A host of other authors have continued to use Cthulhu & Co. in the background material of their own stories; why waste a perfectly good cosmology? The results have ranged from the ridiculous to the excellent, but prove the enduring quality of Lovecraft as mythmaker. In a recent collection of such works, *New Tales of the Cthulhu Mythos* (edited by Ramsey Campbell, and mostly excellent), the major character of one story is purported to have been a friend of Lovecraft's. "Ah, Howard," he muses, "your triumph was complete the moment your name became an adjective."

True. But it is a sad cliché of the creative life that death came to Lovecraft before there was any hint that such adjectival fame would be his; he only saw one of his works printed between book covers rather than in the ephemeral form of magazines, and that was a private publication. (1890–1937)

BRIAN LUMLEY is one of several Britons who have carried on in the Lovecraftian vein quite neatly. (There have been those who also made something of the fact that he was born almost exactly nine months after Lovecraft's death in 1937.) Lumley has used Lovecraft's people (Randolph Carter), places (dear old Miskatonic U.), and things (Cthulhu & Co.) freely, but with such panache that one can't imagine HPL objecting.

His major excursion into this area is with the linked novels of the "Titus Crow" series, which starts out almost classically in an old house on the outskirts of London where a group of scholars are attempting to prevent the breakthrough of Elder horrors from "beyond." However, Lumley dares go where no man has gone (even Lovecraft), and in the later books sends his characters to the awful places in space, time, and dimension from when the horrors come.

There are also several collections of short stories and other novels unconnected to the "Titus Crow" series, such as *Khai of Ancient Khem*, a romp with reincarnation between predynastic Egypt and the present. (b. 1937)

GEORGE MacDONALD, a Scottish Congregationalist minister who was declared a heretic by his own church, had an extraordinary impact on modern fantasy; it might be said that he single-handedly created the so-called Christian mystic line of fantasy.

MacDonald was a devoted Christian who had a burning vision of the underlying truths of his faith; that "goodness" was not an abstraction, but a real, living, objective force, and that conversely, evil was also concrete. He believed that Jesus, in demanding that his followers come to him as little children, meant that one must reject all worldliness and cynicism, and be as innocent, trusting, and full of wonder at life as a child in order to know the Good. He believed that only by surrendering one's will to God (Good) could one achieve true freedom, and that by allowing the evil part of the self to literally die, one could rise again to an earthly paradise. When he was denied the pulpit, MacDonald turned to what he considered the second best way of conveying his message, incidentally proving his own belief that what may seem evil fortune at the time can become a greater good. He wrote fairy tales. A man who might have ended his life as an obscure, forgotten preacher became an immortal myth-maker. His works inspired three men who have carried his faith to millions. Those men are C. S. Lewis, Charles Williams, and J. R. R. Tolkien; if they had an inkling of the truth, they received their hint from MacDonald.

The best of MacDonald's works, where the myth comes through most clearly, are his two adult novels, *Phantastes* and *Lilith*, the short novel *The Wise Woman*, and his three related children's books, *At the Back of the North Wind*, *The Princess and the Goblin*, and *The Princess and Curdie*. These last three are classic fairy tales, the adventures of two children, a princess and a miner's son, in a magical country of goblins and evil beasts. The religious element in them is buried so deeply as to be almost undetectable, forming the foundation of the tale. It is in these books that one first encounters MacDonald's only recurring character —the magical, unbearably beautiful, shape-changing woman who holds all life and love gently in her hands. In *The Wise Woman* we meet the Lady again, this time in a slightly more moralistic tale. The story is about two girls, a princess and a shepherd's daughter, who are each, for different reasons, afflicted with an intolerable selfishness. The Wise Woman takes them both and endeavors to teach them the meaning of humility, duty, and love; highly charged words in this day and age, that are invested by MacDonald with a deeply spiritual meaning.

In *Phantastes*, a book MacDonald wrote for adults, he is more precise in his message, making the book a dry and at times very difficult adventure into Faerie land. *Phantastes* is a journey of self-discovery, as a young man undergoes many trials to burn away all that is base in his soul. There are enchanting passages buried in the metaphysics, for MacDonald chose to use living tree-spirits as his symbols of good and evil. The Lady, too, is present, guarding and guiding the young man.

Last in the sequence is *Lilith*, a lyrical, glowing book which grows as it progresses—from an encounter with a magical world to a shattering statement of MacDonald's own deep faith. The story is about Adam, Eve, and Lilith (Adam's first wife), and how, through the magic of forgiveness and love, even Lilith is reborn to Good. In *Lilith*, at last, the reader is given a hint of who MacDonald's Lady may be—Eve herself, long since forgiven for her early transgressions, now and forever watching over her children.

In addition to these novels, MacDonald wrote many short fairy tales. They are collected in a two-volume set called *Gifts of the Christ Child*.

Despite the power of his works, George MacDonald was not a very good writer. C. S. Lewis wrote:

> If we define Literature as an art whose medium is words, then certainly MacDonald has no place in its first rank—perhaps not even in its second. . . . His writing as a whole is undistinguished, at times, fumbling. . . . But this does not quite dispose of him even for the literary critic. What he does best is fantasy—fantasy that hovers between the allegorical and the mythopoeic. And this, in my opinion, he does better than any man.

MacDonald made myths, myths that send reverberations down the entire life of anyone who has read him. That in itself is quite enough reason to enjoy his tales. (1824–1905)

The tales of ARTHUR MACHEN (rhymes with "blacken") have their genesis in the wooded hills of Wales, where he spent a lonely childhood toward the latter half of the nineteenth century. Later he was to become a journalist in London; the extremes of these two environments—the solitude of one, the sordidness of the other—probably contributed heavily to the characteristic sense of foreboding, low-keyed but powerful, that typifies Machen's writings.

They also provided his settings as exemplified in his two best-known works. *The Great God Pan* is set in the hills of Wales, where ancient powers stir in the forests, eventually leading to the corruption and destruction of a young girl.

103

(Blackwood and Forster were to later write variations on the theme.) On the other hand, Lin Carter has referred to Machen's view of London in his *The Three Imposters* as "Baghdad-on-the-Thames"; this complex "novel" is really a collection of short stories and incidents revolving around life in the city of the time in its more sinister aspects. Several sections of the work, primarily "Novel of the Black Seal" and "Novel of the White Powder" (the latter certainly one of the earliest and most horrifying examples of fiction about drug abuse) can stand alone and have been frequently excerpted for collections.

Machen wrote many short stories, and his novel *The Hill of Dreams* should also be mentioned. Not really fantasy, this semiautobiographical work comes close in a psychological study of a sensitive youth to whom the ancient Roman camp near his village becomes a "hill of dreams." (Readers are warned that there is at least one section involving a dog that is not gratuitously thrown in for effect, as in modern horror fiction, but nevertheless will be hard to take for even the not-so-squeamish.)

Machen's work suffered unwarranted negative reaction for his very tenuous association with Oscar Wilde and his set (it was mostly the fact that Beardsley had illustrated the first edition of *The Great God Pan*) during Wilde's trials and troubles, but interest in it revived in the twentieth century, partially due to Lovecraft's acknowledged debt to Machen. Modern readers will find it very underplayed and sometimes slow as compared to modern horror writings (or those of Lovecraft, for that matter), but the admirer of style and evocative ideas will be well satisfied at the effort. (1863–1947)

It is a rare thing that PATRICIA McKILLIP has done, to write a fantasy trilogy good enough to be compared to Tolkien, and yet to have very little that is Tolkienesque about it. Her "Riddle-Master" books are, in fact, very close to true originals and can be compared to *The Lord of the Rings* only in the broadest sense that they are both set in a magical, created world that is made very real to the reader. The most obvious immediate difference is that while the

Tolkien work is epic, in fact practically defines epic, the McKillip trilogy, though it has its share of battles and high adventure, is almost what might be called a chamber fantasy.

The world of the Riddle-Master is quite limited; we cover it from one end to the other across its handful of countries several times during the story. (And it is, by the way, a continuing story; each book of the three ends with a near cliff-hanger, so be sure the other two are readily available when you start the first.) The cast is relatively small, but consists of sharply defined individuals who are all human, though they come in a large variety (shape-changers, ghosts, sorcerer-kings, etc.).

The world and the narrative, nevertheless, are quite complex; McKillip makes few explanatory condescensions, and the first-time reader will be glad of an enlightening list of people and places which is provided, despite its relative paucity. The style is curiously modern, and sometimes downright funny (not every fantasy has a pig stampede), at times caustically so—Raederle, the sharp-tongued heroine, at one point remarks that: "Having a father flying around in the shape of a crow gives you a certain disregard for appearances."

The first book, *The Riddle-Master of Hed*, introduces us to the hero, Morgon of Hed, and a strangely involuted quest, the object of which neither he nor the reader is quite sure. The second volume, *Heir of Sea and Fire*, is dominated by Raederle and *her* search for Morgon. Finally, *Harpist in the Wind* gives us the end of the quest and not a few surprises. Not much more should be said because the trilogy's texture is all riddles and mysteries, and it should be approached with as little foreknowledge as possible.

There was quite a stretch in quality between this series and the book McKillip published before it, *The Forgotten Beasts of Eld*. The latter is certainly charming and imaginative, in its handling of the tale of a good sorceress, her strange pets, and her eventual involvement in the world of humanity, but its legendary quality gives it a two-dimensional characteristic like that of a lovely but unreal tapestry.

McKillip's other works so far have been definitely for

children, but intelligent and amusing, and one can find (particularly in *The Throme of the Erril of Sheril*) the seeds of her wonderful trilogy in them. (b. 1948)

ROBIN McKINLEY made a more-than-auspicious debut in 1978 with her first novel, *Beauty*. At the time, some felt that yet another novelization of a fairy tale was not exactly needed, but McKinley's deft and charming touch made the novel something special.

It is indeed a retelling of the Marie Leprince de Beaumont tale, "Beauty and the Beast," whose roots go as far back as the story of Cupid and Psyche. McKinley has filled it in with realistic events and valid motivations that make it a full-fledged fantasy without distorting the basic fabric of the classic plot except in a few details.

It is one of those rare works in which all the characters are at least well-meaning and mostly downright likable (including the sisters, who, in one of the small deviations from the original, are just not very perceptive). But it is Beauty who is the prime creation, bright, well read, and with an amusing air of cynicism about the wonders of the Beast's enormous castle. She notes therein a dining table "that might take half an hour to walk around but only ten minutes to walk across," for instance.

And she loves the Beast's library, which contains books yet to be written, and revels in reading Doyle, T. H. White, and "'Rudyard Kipling,' [she] said in despair. 'This is a name?'"

Beauty is altogether charming, and promises much for whatever Robin McKinley serves us in the future.

When JOHN MASEFIELD is mentioned, one inevitably thinks of poems of the sea, and perhaps of the position of Poet Laureate of England. However, few know of his two fantasies, among the most delicious ever written. They are of the rare breed of juveniles that transcend that genre and can be read with delight by adults.

The Midnight Folk are the creatures of a large estate in England on which lives the boy, Kay, under the guardianship of his governess, Sylvia Daisy. It seems that Sylvia

Daisy is a practicing witch, in the best pointed-hat, malevolent tradition; there is also the matter of a large treasure, the loss of which many years ago was the responsibility of Kay's family. Kay's toys and the animals of the estate, domestic and wild, help him solve the mystery of the treasure and fight Sylvia Daisy's pernicious actions. The story is of incredible complexity, and Masefield injects many curious elements such as time travel, a winged horse, the goddess Hecate, living toy animals out of *Pooh*, talking live animals à la *The Wind in the Willows*, and mermaids, and somehow makes it all jell.

The Box of Delights again brings Kay into conflict with Sylvia Daisy, this time aided by Herne the Hunter, King Arthur, and a mysterious Punch-and-Judy man and his delightful dog, Barney. (1878–1967)

RICHARD MATHESON is one of those odd hybrids, a writer of science-horror stories. Not, one hastens to add, the mad-scientist-tries-to-take-over-the-world sort, but genuine horror growing out of a futuristic, or slightly skewed, world. Nearly all of his work is short stories, and he is a master of the form. A memorable (and chilling) example is "Dance of the Dead," about a nightclub where the floor show consists of animated corpses, people whose brains have been destroyed by nerve gas while retaining their motor functions.

Two of his novels can loosely be called fantasy (and just as loosely s-f); *Bid Time Return* is about a man who falls in love with an actress who is long dead, and finds a way to travel back in time to become her lover. *I Am Legend* is a "scientific" exploration of vampires and their place in human society.

Matheson's short stories have been collected under the titles *Shock!*, *Shock II*, *Shock III*, and *The Shores of Space*. Each of these volumes includes both straight s-f and horror. (b. 1926)

The work of WILLIAM MAYNE is usually found at the public library in that strange limbo known as the "young adult" section. This is where you'll find most of the quality writers of fantasy whose protagonists are young. Mayne's leading characters *are* young, and his themes are often fairly basic, but his writing is far from simple. Complex and full of imagery, especially that of nature, it draws the reader smoothly into the atmosphere of the story and the personalities of his characters.

Probably best known of Mayne's work is *Earthfasts*, the quiet and matter-of-fact tale of a drummer boy of two hundred years ago who walks into a cave in search of King Arthur's treasure and out into the present day. He is found by two boys of this time, and helped, but not before his presence has affected the countryside, turning standing stones into giants, or back into giants, and bringing magic into today's world. Mayne plays with this magic, and with shifting time, and seems to be saying that sometimes rationality can't deal with the things that go bump in the night. *It* is another of Mayne's novels, again a story of a link through time, but this one is a frightening book, as chilling as it is witty in its telling of a girl who is touched by It, and must find out when, and who or what, It is.

Look through that young-adult section; among other fine writers there, you'll find William Mayne. (b. 1928)

The great A. MERRITT is generally known as a fantasist, but curiously enough, only one of his eight completed novels (two were unfinished at his death) can be described as pure fantasy. Four are given enough scientific basis to be considered science fiction, and three are concerned with the occult and its investigation.

These are *Seven Footprints to Satan*, in which a master criminal with occult powers aims at world domination; *Burn, Witch, Burn!*, about a doll-maker whose creations come alive with malevolent intent; and *Creep, Shadow!*, in which the Demoiselle Dahut d'Ys, certainly one of the most elegantly named villainesses in literature (Ys is a sunken city on the coast of France, overwhelmed by the sea in medieval times for its sorceries), lives again in modern times and attempts to revive the blasphemous practices of the past.

The one pure fantasy, *The Ship of Ishtar*, is one of the

most lushly beautiful ever written, and a sort of touchstone for romantic fantasies of its kind. John Kenton, a contemporary archeologist, under the influence of a strange stone found in the ruins of Babylon, finds himself in another world ruled by the gods of that ancient culture. He is a galley slave on a ship condemned to roam the seas of that world forever, on which Ishtar and Nergal, deities of love and evil, struggle eternally for domination. Kenton's presence on the ship destroys the balance, and he is precipitated into wild adventures, accompanied by Sharane, priestess of Ishtar, another of Merritt's vividly exotic women.

There may be no more breathtaking scene in fantasy than the one in which Kenton enters the temple of Bel, the levels of which are each dedicated to a god of the Babylonian pantheon; each manifests itself as Kenton ascends.

This overripe (to some), rich (to others) beauty also pervades Merritt's handful of short stories, the most notable of which, "The Woman of the Wood," brings a dryad into contemporary times. The shorter works have been collected in *The Fox Woman and Other Stories*.

Merritt's work is considered pop pulp fantasy by many, but his stories have enchanted and intrigued for over half a century, and will probably continue to do so. (1889–1943)

The reputation of HOPE MIRRLEES rests on a single novel, *Lud-in-the-Mist*. It was published at a time (1926) when the dedicated reader of fantasy had very few books from which to choose, and even fewer set "beyond the fields we know," in Dunsany's felicitous phrase. Therefore each precious example that came along made its mark and established its own small cult. Today some of these suffer in comparison to the best of the relatively vast quantity of fantasy available. *Lud-in-the-Mist* is one of these, but its tale of a small pastoral community, very like one that might be found in the Shire, and its battle against the influences of Faerie, which lies across the Elfin Marches and the Debatable Hills, is still charmingly readable. (1887–1978)

NAOMI MITCHISON is one of those women of protean talent that England seems to produce; a list of her skills and accomplishments makes amazing reading. It is only with her writing that we are concerned here; little known in the United States, she is famed in England for her historical fiction, compared by connoisseurs to the best of Graves and Renault. She has written at least two excellent science-fiction novels, but her major work of fantasy is *To the Chapel Perilous*.

In this novel, Mitchison meets T. H. White on his own ground—generally, the anachronistic historical novel, the fantasy elements being the anachronisms; specifically, the Arthurian novel—and the results are at the least a draw. *To the Chapel Perilous* recounts the quest for the Grail as seen through the eyes of the reporters for the local news media. If this sounds unutterably whimsical, forget it. Out of her broad anthropological background, Mitchison evokes primordially unpleasant forces—the Old Religion vs. Christianity—that can make the hair stand on end. Short but powerful, it's an extraordinary tour de force that has never seen publication in the U.S.

At least one of her historical novels also deserves mention. *The Corn King and the Spring Queen* (unfortunately retitled *The Barbarian* in the U.S.) is a monumental, complex work contrasting the cultures of post-Alexandrian Sparta and "barbarian" Scythia (with a really nasty conclusion in Hellenistic Egypt). Part of the Scythian culture is, very simply, magic, very much underplayed, but pictured as totally incomprehensible to the civilized mind.

The works of Naomi Mitchison, no matter what the category, will amply repay the search to find them that is necessary, particularly in America. (b. 1897)

RICHARD MONACO's offbeat Arthurian trilogy, *Parsival, The Grail War*, and *The Final Quest*, is one part Mallory, one part *Candide*, and one part *The Sotweed Factor*, all blended together by the author's acute eye for the inherent absurdities of the human condition.

The books tell the story of Parsival, a young man with severe emotional problems. He was raised (as in the legends) on a remote kingdom, sheltered by his mother from all contact with the world, war, and men. The poor lad doesn't really know who or what he is, but he *has* heard about knights, and decides that he wants to be one. So off he goes, with his mother's most grudging blessing, to join the court at Camelot and become a knight. It turns out that the boy is incredibly strong, pure of heart (translation: unbelievably naïve), and just what is needed for the Grail Quest.

The narrative is fast-paced, occasionally coarse, and ranges from the grim to the bitterly ironic. If you would like to keep your illusions about the flowering of knighthood, Monaco's tales are not for you. If, on the other hand, you never quite believed it all anyway, give them a try. (b. 1940)

When MICHAEL MOORCOCK began his now labyrinthine sword-and-sorcery series with the publication of *The Stealer of Souls*, he started something new. Up to that point, the subgenre had been very heavy on the swords, and the sorcery was chiefly put to use to inconvenience the human hero. With the creation of Elric of Melnibone, Moorcock gave the world of fantasy truly *magical* sword-and-sorcery. Elric is the albino Emperor of the Sorcerer kingdom of Melnibone, an unhuman realm, worshiping the demon Gods of Chaos and with dominion over Men. Elric more or less enlists on the side of Law, but is bound to a demon-sword from which he draws his strength. This situation sets up awesome conflicts, and Elric is one of the most tortured, lonely, and guilt-ridden heroes ever to grace the pages of fiction.

The series is labyrinthine because it is intimately tied up with Moorcock's Eternal Champion cycle. The Eternal Champion is something of a Platonic Absolute, a heroic figure that appears in many places and times, with many aspects and names. One aspect is Elric, another is Dorian Hawkmoon of the "Runestaff" series (more sword-and-sorcery) and the "Castle Brass" series (although technically Castle Brass could be considered particularly baroque science fiction). The Eternal Champion is Erikose from

The Silver Warriors, Prince Corum in the "Chronicles of Corum"; he is also Jerik Carnelian in the "End of Time" series, which is mostly science fiction, and therefore Jerry Cornelius, from a series of books which is clearly s-f. (Moorcock is a prolific writer!) All of these series interlock in a sort of four-dimensional superseries which is marked by consistently high-quality narrative prose and inventive plotting.

Moorcock turned from sword-and-sorcery to a more ornate and glittering form of fantasy with *Gloriana*; this is a novel set in an alternate England, and, like Peake's "Gormenghast" series, the magic is all in the atmosphere. Gloriana is the ruler of Albion, and, like her model, Queen Elizabeth I, her ministers are scheming to marry her off. Intrigue and manipulation fill the book, and the Queen in the end calls a halt by marrying the man who was best able to control the others. In this book Moorcock has revealed a remarkable ability to build an atmosphere with a few well-chosen words, to characterize in a sentence, and to create a complex, bizarre, yet wholly believable world. The palace Gloriana inhabits is many palaces, built around, on top of, beneath, and beside each other. It is a maze. Living within the walls is an entire secondary court of escaped prisoners, beggars, thieves, fugitives, and madmen. Each character has his or her own secret rooms and passages. In fact, the structure of the building mirrors the structure of the plot; the relationships between characters are echoed in the juxtaposition of their rooms. *Gloriana* is a book to be savored and read slowly, the better to enjoy every nuance of Moorcock's craft. (b. 1939)

C. L. MOORE's Jirel of Joiry stories, collected in *The Black God's Shadow* and scattered through Moore's other collections, are sword-and-sorcery with an emphasis on sorcery, despite the heroine's manifest proficiency with a sword. Jirel is the fiery lady of Castle Joiry, which, like its mistress, is more than it seems. Deep in the nethermost dungeon of the citadel lies an entrance to Hell; Jirel is caught in a web of treachery that forces her to enter again and again.

112

Moore's Hell is a frighteningly well realized nightmare world, where the horrors are not dancing demons with pitchforks but the manifest terrors of the human subconscious: ghostly horses race weeping across a dark plain, and the hideous shadows of naked trees reach out to ensnare the unwary.

Writing between 1934 and 1939, Moore created and developed a character so rich and human that it comes almost as a shock to realize that there are only six stories. Like Robert E. Howard, Moore created her fantasy world by giving the reader only glimpses of it, and implied an epic life for Jirel while telling only of brief moments. Much early sword-and-sorcery has been lost entirely, or blurred by those who came after, explaining and expanding the work. Jirel still stands alone, untouched by the revisionists, a monument to the spare and graceful art form that sword-and-sorcery was at its inception.

Most of C. L. Moore's work is s-f, but her style of writing and her choice of characters and setting always has a strong fantasy flavor; these other books, and particularly *Judgment Night*, should not be overlooked by the fantasy reader. (b. 1911)

Though fairly well known in the science-fiction field, JOHN MORRESEY is new to the fantasy genre, and his debut work was, if not a classic of its kind, at least an extremely imaginative use of familiar elements. There are the three boys, and the dying father who tells them of their inheritance in a far land. In *Ironbrand* there is a prophecy, suitably cryptic, uttered by a suitably mysterious prophet, and there is sufficient magic and mayhem for most any taste, as well as a deft touch and a sense of humor, making it a harbinger of Morresey's probable popularity in fantasy. (b. 1930)

WILLIAM MORRIS is a problem. He is vitally important to the history of fantasy fiction, but many modern readers will find his work virtually unreadable. His historical importance is touched on elsewhere in this book; here we are concerned with what the fantasy aficionado will find on

113

tackling a Morris novel; it must be reported that, alas, he or she will find the need for patience and perseverance.

Why this may be can be explained by the fact that Morris was writing in the late Victorian age. The literature-reading public of that age had two advantages on us. One was a great deal of time, undistracted by such things as television, in which to read long, stylized novels. The other was an ability to cope with that stylization, since many literary works, in their language and the way it was used, were far from the language of every day; many of the books of the time were as artificially constructed and as "unrealistic" as a Pre-Raphaelite painting—in the manner in which they were written.

Morris was, of course, *the* Renaissance man of the nineteenth century. He was accomplished and/or influential in architecture, sculpture, writing (prose and poetry), music, social philosophy (he was one of the first voices raised against environmental damage perpetrated by industry), and the design of glass, furniture, fabrics, and wallpaper. He was one of the originators of the Pre-Raphaelite movement, and he is regarded by many, and with good cause, as the inventor of the fantasy novel. His three major works in that vein show a kinship with the Pre-Raphaelite painters in the preoccupation with a sort of medieval mysticism. The three (*The Water of the Wondrous Isles, The Well at the World's End,* and *The Wood beyond the World*) are also highly stylized in their writing, a sort of artificial English attempting to evoke what English would have been in the Middle Ages had it been a good deal more like what it is today in vocabulary.

And there, of course, lies the difficulty for the modern reader. But if that reader has some of that Victorian patience and perseverance, he will be rewarded with wonderful stories, of journeys and quests through unknown lands, of strange and fey creatures, of sorceresses and knights and princes, of mystical wells and woods and isles, all taking place in worlds that for the first time were totally created, that bore no link to our own in history or geography.

Perhaps the best reason for attempting a novel by William Morris is that given for attempting Mt. Everest —because it is there. (1834–1896)

TALBOT MUNDY is generally considered to be a writer of historical adventure, such as the famous and oft-mentioned *King of the Khyber Rifles*, but when a writer is working with an historical period or a culture where belief in the supernatural is common and strong, a few wizards and demons may well creep into the story. This, and the wonderful sense of adventure and excitement, is what draws fantasy readers to most of his novels. There is, though, a series of novels that are more properly described as fantasy, rather than historical, adventures. These numerous books relate the activities of James Schuyler Grim (Jimgrim) as he and a band of cohorts fight the forces of the occult in India. One of the earliest of the Doc Savage ilk, Jimgrim is a steely-eyed, firm-jawed hero of the first water and the sheer number of books about his exploits is enough alone to recommend him to series fanatics, though the style may be a little dated for modern tastes. (1879–1940)

H. WARNER MUNN is perhaps best known for his stories about Merlin and his godson Gwalchmai, as told in *King of the World's Edge*, *The Ship from Atlantis*, and *Merlin's Godson*. In this wildly imaginative set of novels, the action starts just after Arthur's last battle, with Merlin and a Roman soldier, along with assorted adventurers, leaving Britain to travel to new lands. One of their first new lands turns out to be what is now known as Florida, where they are captured by Indians and rescued by a chap named Hayonwatha (sound familiar?) who takes them to another group of Indians—who may be the mound-builders—who put them in the equivalent of a dungeon from which they escape to go with Hayonwatha to some more Indians in the Northwest and they set up a confederation of tribes and take revenge and then go into the Southwest where they run into still *more* Indians, these being Mians and Aztlans, and then they ... And that's only part of the first book. The next two novels detail the globe-and-time-spanning adventures of Gwalchmai and his star-crossed (and recrossed and ...) lover, Corenice.

Lesser known but possibly more interesting is the series

of stories begun with "The Werewolf of Ponkert." This first story, set in fifteenth-century Hungary, tells of the capture of a man named Wladislaw Brenryk by a werepack whose leader is one known only as "the master." After running with the pack for a time, Brenryk attempts escape, and the stories that follow describe the master's revenge on his family down through the centuries. (1903–1981)

ROBERT NATHAN is best known for writing the sort of gentle fantasy verging on whimsy that was so popular in the 1930s and '40s. But there is also sensitivity and a touch of acidity to be found in his stories. For instance, in the *Journey of Tapiola*, the title character, a Yorkshire terrier, sets out to be a hero because "much of his life was spent in such places as behind the sofa." He is accompanied by a canary named Richard (which he prefers to "Dickie"), and one might judge that the novel could well be a sticky, saccharine piece of cuteness. But it is surprisingly succinct, even terse, and has surprises such as the rat Jeremiah, who fancies himself a religious prophet and is far from cute. *Portrait of Jennie* tells of a young painter who paints the portrait of a mysterious girl who is a child when he first meets her, but who grows to womanhood in the short time he takes to paint her.

In *The Bishop's Wife*, an angel comes to Earth to correct a bishop's erring ways; in *The Mallot Diaries*, Neanderthal man survives into the present day with tragic results; and in *The Fair*, there is one of the first attempts to have a bit of fun with the Arthurian legends.

Nathan's works are out of fashion now, but they are small jewels that more than repay seeking them out in libraries and used-book stores. (b. 1894)

The vast importance of EDITH NESBIT to the history of fantasy, not to mention science fiction, has not really been acknowledged, but the evidence is there for those who look. It should certainly seem obvious that there is *something* special about an author known only for her works for children whose undiminished popularity is now well into its fourth quarter of a century.

Much of Nesbit's writing was done for the children's magazines of the day, which accounts for the sometimes episodic character of her stories. She was an all-around remarkable woman; there is some speculation as to an affair with the young George Bernard Shaw before her marriage, and her friendship with H. G. Wells was of very long duration. She, too, was a Fabian Socialist.

What were the qualities that characterized her stories, which were usually about families of children, sometimes two siblings, sometimes as many as six, who would come upon a magic being or artifact (in one case a garden), resulting inevitably in totally delightful chaos?

For one thing, the children are wonderfully real; they are not the little prigs of most Victorian juvenile literature; they are certainly nice, and very bright, but given a magic carpet, their inventive mischief with such an object is awe-inspiring.

And as for inventive, Nesbit's magic is most original, hinting of great wonder and strangeness in the background but manifesting itself in very unorthodox forms. There is the psammead, an extremely literal-minded sand fairy who grants wishes; the aforementioned magic carpet, which comes complete with a most talkative and conceited phoenix; an erratic magic ring that causes utter confusion until it is realized that its magic is anything you say it is; and an amulet in the form of a horseshoe that grows into a gateway to the past and the future.

Even adult readers will find a good many laughs in Nesbit's work; her humor is not only in her children's view of the world in general and the adult world in particular, but in the disastrous results that the most innocent attempts to manipulate magic seem to precipitate. There are the five children wishing to be "beautiful as the day" and the awful unrecognizability it engenders, the maid who borrows the enchanted ring and is suddenly invisible on her afternoon out with the best beau, and the highly indignant Queen of Babylon who invades the British Museum demanding all of her property back.

If this were all there was to Nesbit's writing, it would be considered a charming and readable relic of the Victorian age. But there is one other factor, a very important and rather subtle one, and that is consistency. That may seem minor, but one of the author's major tasks in fantasy is to render his/her imaginative creations believable. Most fantasies, until about the turn of the century when Nesbit was writing, were of the surrealist Alice-in-Wonderland type, where absolutely anything could appear out of left field to keep the plot (if any) going, or the mystical-quest fantasies of William Morris, more "realistic" in a way, but nevertheless still fairly illogical on many points.

Not only did Nesbit set her tales in the ultrareal here-and-now of her readers, but her stories of magic were absolutely consistent. Once the magic person, place, or thing had been found and its rules established, everything that happened grew out of this, and no new fantasy elements were added for any reason. Could it be mere coincidence that her close friend H. G. Wells was establishing some fundamental rules of science fiction along the same lines? And certainly, the millions of children who have read and loved her books over the years must have included the Inklings (Tolkien, Williams, and Lewis), as well as most of the writers who have made their mark in fantasy in this century. (The hero of Michael Moorcock's *The Warlord of the Air* is Oswald Bastable, who is the narrator of Nesbit's only major nonfantasy, the trilogy collectively called *The Bastables*.)

Nesbit's best stories are generally considered to be the "Five Children" trilogy (sometimes to be found in one volume, but more often published as three: *The Five Children and It*, "it" being the sand-fairy psammead, *The Phoenix and the Carpet*, and *The Story of the Amulet*) and *The Enchanted Castle*. The latter contains her most transcendentally conceived moments of beauty, as when all the statues of the enormous grounds of the castle come alive on an enchanted moonlit night, and of terror (a quality seldom found in her work), when a group of hastily made dummies becomes animate and persists in acting like a group of perfectly normal people.

Other works of almost equal delight are *Wet Magic* (a kingdom of merfolk), *The Magic Garden* (in which one learns a good deal about the language of flowers, but never really whether the garden is truly magical), and *The House of Arden* and its sequel, *Harding's Luck*, in which is met the magical mouldiwarp.

Nesbit's importance in the history of fantasy, whatever it may have been, is still secondary to the enchantment of her books themselves. They will continue to enthrall readers, probably forever. (1858–1924)

LARRY NIVEN, one of the best of the high-tech science-fiction writers, has ventured comparatively little into the fantasy field; when he does it's usually with scientifically reasoned stories. "The Flight of the Horse," for instance, is the title story in a collection of short tales about time travel: Svetz, a man of the very far future, is sent on errands through time by his autocratic master. This would seem to be science fiction, as a machine is used, but when Svetz goes for a dog he comes back with a werewolf; sent to find a horse, he returns with one that has a horn on its forehead. These stories are slyly humorous and most enjoyable. One of them, "What Good Is a Glass Dagger?" introduces the concept of "mana," that which makes magic possible. This idea is explored in more detail in *The Magic Goes Away*, in which a band of travelers, guided by a wizard's skull, seek the source of magic and attempt to return it to the world. This novella, with its vivid characterization and touch of humor, is curiously poignant.

Inferno, co-written with Jerry Pournelle, is a modernized version of Dante's classic, with a science-fiction writer the one who goes to Hell. There is high humor and satire in this one, with jibes at contemporary customs, mores, heroes, and villains. There is also a delightful scene at the tomb of a well-known writer. *Inferno*'s not Dante, but it is a lot of fun. (b. 1938)

One of the most interesting, if well done, of the fantasy subgenres is that of time travel, and DIANA NORMAN's *Fitzempress' Law* (1980) is one of the best. The plot is fairly simple—three young English toughs, two male and one female, harass and assault an old woman, and she uses her powers as a witch to send them back to a time when there was no real law and order, to see if they can develop a little respect for same—but Ms. Norman's evocation of the historical period (twelfth century, with Henry II ruling), and of the social strata (peasant, knight, and nun) into which the protagonists are thrown, make this a fascinating novel. And if the premise sounds a little moral, it is—but the moral is not what you may think.

ELIZABETH NORMAN is primarily a writer of romances, gothic and otherwise, and this shows in *Silver, Jewels and Jade* (1980), particularly in the first three chapters. We have the handsome prince, the beautiful maiden, and the stepsister who is selfish and hates the beautiful maiden. Then Ms. Norman begins adding more and more fantasy elements and the reader is slowly moved from a straight romance to a fascinating "pre-Arthurian" fantasy.

JOAN NORTH. "If you can hold in your hand the Lightstone and hear in the silence the true note that is yourself, then you will be able to enter the Maze." This quote from one of her books seems to express Joan North's approach to fantasy. The mental and spiritual attitudes of her protagonists influence greatly their success or failure.

In *The Cloud Forest* Andrew Badger, a twelve-year-old orphan forced to live with a domineering aunt in an English girls' school, finds a strange ring with a lovely milky stone. Through this ring and his dreams, Andrew is able to enter the haven of the Cloud Forest, a place of shifting shapes of trees and wisps of bushes. The forest and the friendship of Ronnie Peters, a young girl of strong and original mind, combine to help him overcome the evil forces ranged in pursuit of the power of the ring, and to find his rightful heritage.

The Whirling Shapes, loosed from another place by the imagination of an eccentric old lady and the anguish of a young artist, feed on the mechanical in humanity, the joyless automatic reactions of people who will not allow creativity to flourish, in themselves or others. A young girl's own imagination and courage allow her to force the shapes back through the door of the strange house that keeps appearing and disappearing on the heath. An implication here is that being staid is almost as bad as being dead.

The Light Maze, from which the above quote is taken, is an exciting examination of the nature of illusion and reality and their effects on time, space, and matter. The plot is relatively simple: Tom Nancarrow disappears while doing research on the legend of the Lightstone, an apparently magical object prominent in local myth. It is not until two years later that Kit, twenty-year-old godchild of Tom's wife Sally, comes to stay and finds the clues, and the serenity, that enable her to enter the shimmering, glistening maze of light and find Tom. North does nice things within this structure, however. Comparative religion, the power of the subconcious, and the importance of knowing oneself are only a few of the topics she manages to weave into the novel.

All in all, though North's subject matter may be a bit basic for some tastes, her visual imagery is a reward in itself, with her forests and shapes and shining tigers and serpents and, of course, the Light Maze. (b. 1920)

More of ANDRE NORTON's work is in science fiction than in fantasy, but when authors are as prolific as Ms. Norton, even their minority genre comprises many books. Her "Witch World" series is an example: it is a science-fictional series, with most of the "magic" explained by extrasensory abilities, but three of the twelve books are almost pure fantasy. In these three she concentrates on the Wereriders of Witch World, people who can change to animals by an act of will. *The Year of the Unicorn* is the time set when the Lords of High Hallack must pay the Wereriders for their help in battle: thirteen brides must be offered, thirteen women who will leave their homes to live in the Wasteland with the riders. One of these women is Gillan, a foundling, and the thrust of the story is her search for her identity, both actually and metaphorically. *The Crystal Gryphon* and *The Jargoon Pard* also use the riders, and, like *Unicorn,* are high romantic fantasy.

Norton's children's fantasy is enjoyable only by children and adults who really like children's fantasy. Most of these books have similar themes—youth, confused and hurt through loneliness, "being different," racism, or some other problem, finds strength and self through magic. Best of these is *Fur Magic*, which offers an exciting look at Amerindian magic. Others include *Octagon Magic*, *Dragon Magic*, *Steel Magic*, and *Lavender-Green Magic*, this last being a particularly well written and constructed time-travel fantasy.

Huon of the Horn is unusual for Ms. Norton in that it's pure fantasy *and* adult fantasy. It is an evocative retelling of a part of the Charlemagne saga, in which Huon is banished from the court of Charlemagne and eventually finds refuge in the court of Oberon, in Faerie. There is action, adventure, love, and glory. What more could one ask? (b. 1912)

In his work in the fantasy field, ANDREW OFFUTT seems to specialize in adding to the typical sword-and-sorcery novel a few extra ingredients, such as sex (the violence has always been there), humor, and a general worldliness.

Some of Offutt's novels (*Ardor on Aros* and *Chieftain of Andor*), while technically science fiction similar to the Burroughs "Mars" series, would probably be enjoyed by most fantasy fans for their action and tongue-in-cheek style. In the vein of purer fantasy is a series starring Robert E. Howard's hero, Cormac Mac Art, a mighty Irish swordsman, legend and bane of evil sorcerers. And there is the delightful series centered on the talented and lovely Tiana of Reme, illegitimate daughter of a duke and foster child of a slightly sleazy pirate captain, Caranga. Written in collaboration with Richard Lyon, this trilogy owes a debt, and adds a bit (mostly sex and a delightfully smart-ass sense of humor) to C. L. Moore's Jirel of Joiry stories. Though not really a supreme egomaniac, Tiana does have a profound confidence in her own beauty, intelligence, and physical prowess, and all these attributes are needed in her adventures as she battles the wizards, demons, and other supernatural, and natural, horrors that litter her path. In the premiere novel, *The Demon in the Mirror*, Tiana is questing, but to this quest Offutt adds his own macabre humor—the search is for the various parts of a dead wizard's body, and interesting characters abound, prominent among them Caranga and a wizard with the paradoxical name Pyre of Ice. This series is highly recommended for those who like Jirel, or Leiber's characters, Fafhrd and the Gray Mouser. (b. 1937)

ALEXI PANSHIN, with his wife CORY, wrote a single fantasy novel, *Earthmagic*. This is a traditional coming-of-age fantasy that relies heavily on the legends surrounding the Old Religion.

The protagonist of the book, Haldane, is the young son and heir of a chieftain whose people invaded the land of the goddess Libera. The goddess's people are oppressed and enslaved, but her power is too great to be entirely suppressed. When Haldane's father is killed in battle, the boy finds that he has been chosen by Libera to unite the two peoples into one, with himself as king.

Most of the book describes Haldane's dual struggle to gain his birthright and come to terms with his destiny as a goddess's consort. On a deeper level, *Earthmagic* is about the power of the land and the need humans have to know it intimately, to be a part of it. (b. 1940)

The genius of MERVYN PEAKE defies encapsulization. There is no way to convey the strangeness and beauty of his people and places, the grotesquerie of his plots and events, the searing pictures his writing leaves in the reader's mind.

This extraordinary individuality, these novels that defy description, owe something to the fact that before Peake was a writer he was a painter and illustrator. His paintings have received serious notice in the art world; the books he illustrated (mostly during the 1940s) are now collectors' items. The illustrations he did for the two Alice books are initially startling, but many feel they are the only ones that can seriously rival Tenniel's.

And before Peake wrote fiction he wrote poetry; several volumes were published, again to serious consideration by the critics.

The painter's eye, the poet's ear, go to make up Peake's prose. But if you're thinking in terms of dull, intellectual artiness, think again. Peake's masterpiece is the towering "Gormenghast" trilogy, which has enough bloodcurdling moments and intrigue for any number of John Le Carré novels.

There is also passion, love, hate, madness, and humor (albeit rather macabre humor). And the fantastic thing is that in the first two novels of the trilogy, *Titus Groan* and *Gormenghast*, nothing fantastic happens. There are no otherworldly creatures evoked; no magic is performed; no event is beyond the mundane ken. But the world of Gormenghast is a created world, with no links to the world we know, and its inhabitants are so fantastic in themselves and in the life of ritual that they lead that there are few works more qualified to be considered a high point of imaginative fiction.

Gormenghast is a castle, an enormous castle of endless rooms, courts, passages, roofs, stairways, and attics. It is a microcosm to the macrocosm of Middle-Earth, for instance. Vast numbers of people live there, some involved in its daily life, some totally removed. The events of *Titus Groan* and *Gormenghast* take place almost entirely within its walls; those that don't are close to them.

The ruling family is the focus of the two novels. There is Sepulchrave, the seventy-sixth Earl of Groan, subject to melancholia and madness; Gertrude, his wife, who moves always on and among a carpet of white cats; the adolescent Fuchsia, their daughter, who dreams away her life in an attic full of old toys; and Titus, the son whose birth opens the first novel, whose first birthday closes it, whose eventful boyhood is the substance of the second.

There are the mad twin aunts, Cora and Clarisse, who finish each other's sentences, live in a room of roots, and lust for power; the servants and retainers; and always, weaving through their lives creatively and destructively, the ex-scullion Steerpike, who escapes from the kitchens on the day of Titus's birth and attempts to change the order of Gormenghast forever.

Without Peake's prose, this all sounds like a castleful of English eccentrics; with it, the reader is pulled into a circumscribed world where every moment leaves indelible images not easily forgotten. Reading these novels is, quite literally, an experience.

The third novel, *Titus Alone*, is in another key entirely. Here Titus leaves Gormenghast and makes his way in an outside world, equally bizarre but more diffuse. It must be read, of course, by those who respond to the first two of the trilogy, but like life itself, it is a withdrawal from the initial intensity of youth.

Peake's other fiction includes a book for children, *Captain Slaughterboard Drops Anchor*, that needed some pretty sophisticated kiddies to appreciate it, and a curious fable for adults, *Mr. Pye*, about a mild-mannered gentleman who sprouts angelic wings or devilish horns depending on his momentary nature, an amusingly whimsical variation on the Jekyll-and-Hyde theme.

One other work of Peake's fiction must be mentioned, a novelette entitled *Boy in Darkness*. It is apparently an incident in Titus's life that occurs between *Titus Groan* and *Gormenghast*; where the novels are written with a bright, clear light like that of a painter's studio, this shorter work is spare, cloudy, and surrealist, singularly frightening in its depiction of a boy's encounter with sinister beasts (especially a lamb of terrifying intensity) in a setting of arid monochromaticism.

And it might be unnecessary to point out that those editions of Peake's work with his own illustrations are doubly impressive; perhaps not since Blake has an artist of such talent written with such talent.

Peake's work has been slow but sure in making its mark, and now the influence is being felt. The startlingly original fantasies of Jane Gaskell still show that she has visited Gormenghast; Michael Moorcock's glorious *Gloriana* is dedicated to Peake with good reason. Mervyn Peake will inevitably be listed among this century's foremost creative artists. (1911–1968)

The works of EDGAR ALLAN POE hold many surprises for the reader of fantasy who is unfamiliar with them. He wrote stories that contain much humor and warmth, as well as the gloomy masterpieces of horror for which he is best remembered. Poe was a versatile writer, who holds a title in many literary genres as one of the first practitioners. Many people call him the Founding Father of Fantasy, although a search for pure fantasy in his work is surprisingly inconclusive.

Poe was an intellectual in the best sense of the word, extremely well read in the latest scientific discoveries. Many of his stories which seem most magical also lend themselves to logical interpretation. "The Case of M. Valdemar," in which a dying man's corpse putrefies when loosed from a hypnotic trance, is only a little beyond the science of Poe's day. "William Wilson," a terrifying story of a man haunted by his *doppelgänger*, may be, like "The Telltale Heart," only the hallucination of a psychotic mind.

Even Poe's most mystical stories are grounded in a single philosophical principle of his time: that the identity or will is a thing apart from the body, which persists after death. This manifests itself in the theme of premature burial, a motif so common in Poe's short stories that it becomes a sort of recurring nightmare. *The Fall of the House of Usher*, in some ways the archetypal Poe story, tells of a beautiful, pale young woman wasting away and entombed before her death. *Usher* contains an equivocal fantasy touch, as the dreary old mansion collapses in sympathy with the death of its Lord and Lady. Later stories, including "Ligeia," "Berenice," "Eleonora," and "Morella," are variations on the theme, introducing the notion of reincarnation or possession, as a departed beloved takes on the form of a successor.

Poe's most successful stories are spare, vivid, and evocative, as in his later years he abandoned the elaborate language which slowed his earlier works. These include "Hop Frog," "King Pest," with its delightfully horrible collection of ghouls, and "The Masque of the Red Death," perhaps his finest work. Pure fantastic imagery dominates many brief sketches, and transcends meaning entirely in his poems: "The Haunted Palace," "Ulalume," and "The City in the Sea."

It is a pleasant surprise to discover that Poe also wrote warm, wry, and amusing fantasy stories. Two of the best are "Never Bet the Devil Your Head" and "Bon-Bon," both classic pact-with-the-devil tales. Another, "Some Words with a Mummy," is a devastating satire on nineteenth-century progress. And, in "A Predicament," Poe deftly burlesques all the morbid excess of his own early work.

Poe's contribution to fantasy lies less in his choice of subject matter than in his masterful control of atmosphere. His sense of the mysterious and macabre is as acute in rational tales such as *The Narrative of Arthur Gordon Pym* as in his works of overt horror. In fact, all the clichés of modern horror—the sable drapes and blood-red carpets, sickly damsels and dripping candelabra, cobwebbed tombs and grinning death's-heads, were Poe's creations. His virtuoso technique influenced not only Lovecraft, Machen, Bloch, and Bradbury, but Rimbaud, Baudelaire, and generations of literate symbolists all over the world. (1809–1849)

TIM POWERS. Humor in fantasy is relatively common, ranging from the clever to the absurd. *The Drawing of the Dark* (1979) manages to cover most of this spectrum while telling a vigorous story of high fantasy full of engaging characters and exciting events. Part of the humor is derived from wordplay, clever and subtle, and the title itself leads to one of the most outrageous, and surprising, puns on paper.

Brian Duffy, a battle-weary soldier, is hired by an old man to go to Vienna and act as bouncer in a small inn. Simple enough. But from the moment the oldster lights up a dried snake and smokes it, Brian and the reader are in for rousing adventure and delightful fantasy. Too much plot revelation will spoil the many surprises, but suffice to say that the time is early sixteenth century, there is a wizard named Ambrosius, whom fans of Arthurian fantasy will recognize, Suleiman is attacking from the East, and there are some Vikings running around worrying about Ragnarok. All in all a marvelous work.

FLETCHER PRATT is now primarily known as the successful collaborator of L. Sprague de Camp—successful in the sense that while each was very much his own voice, in combination yet a third writer emerged, equally as good but separate. This Spraguenfletcher, as he might be called, wrote those outrageous tall *Tales from Gavagan's Bar* and the Harold Shea stories, which lie smack between fantasy and science fiction, but delight the lover of fantasy in particular, since they take place in worlds built around works of myth and fiction. (They're also pretty funny fare.)

But the individual writer, Fletcher Pratt, has to his credit two amazing novels, *The Well of the Unicorn* and *The Blue Star*. Both are excellent fantasy, but they are amazing because of when they appeared (*Well* in 1948, *Star* in 1952). Fantasy readers of today are spoiled in the sense of having a great number of works to choose from (good, bad, and indifferent, of course, and never enough for the addict). When the two Pratt novels appeared, their antecedents were minimal to the point of nonexistence: William Morris's mystically medieval novels, Leiber's Gray Mouser stories, Howard's Conan canon, and an odd little juvenile from England called *The Hobbit*.

So out of almost nowhere came *The Well of the Unicorn*, which certainly baffled readers of the time. Pratt was noted as a historian; this novel reads like a scholarly work of historical fiction by an author with a flair for the dramatic. The fantasy elements are strong (wizards, trolls, the magic well itself), but are curiously underplayed—they are simply a part of this world as are the landscapes, the various cultures, the emotional relationships between the extremely well drawn characters.

The novel is very dense; it has its share of action, but that is no more its *raison d'être* than the fantasy elements. The medieval background, political and cultural, is enormously complicated, and the reader is thrown into it, to sink or swim. The large cast is exquisitely characterized; there is the naïve but bright hero, Airar; the ambiguous sorcerer, Meliboe (a sort of uninvolved Gandalf); the five star captains of Carrhoene, one of whom is female; and the varied royal siblings, Aurea, Argyra, and Aurareus. (As is evident, Pratt was blessed with the gift of nomenclature.)

In *The Blue Star*, also, magic is a fact of life in the novel's parallel universe, in a world physically similar to Earth, but socially different. And no heroic fantasy this, either; the historical analogue to the background of *The Blue Star* is more eighteenth century than eighth—a quite civilized but crumbling Empire with more bureaucrats than barbarians. The magic here is a rare talent, inherited in the female line; what's more, it is frowned upon by the state religion. Nevertheless, it is useful to politicians and revolutionaries, of which there is a plenitude since the Empire is nearing a state of chaos. Rodvard, a young clerk, is manipulated by a revolutionary group into seducing the young witch-to-be, Lalette—she will only acquire her powers when no longer a virgin. From there, the two spend their time escaping from and succumbing to the various power groups that wish to use Lalette's skills.

The Blue Star is cynical, dour, introverted, and as much a novel of character as of action, a rare quality in fantasy. It and *The Well of the Unicorn* were extraordinary for their time, and are still very special in the field. (1897–1956)

A uniquely American style of fantasy developed in the first decades of the twentieth century, and E. HOFFMAN PRICE was squarely in the middle of the movement, even though he himself was not a master. This was the era of the pulps: adventure, detective, horror, science fiction, and just plain weird fiction magazines flourished. Young writers named Lovecraft, Howard, Brackett, and Smith were making their names. But if one judges by sheer volume of published work, E. Hoffman Price was more popular than any of them. Between 1923 and 1952 Price sold more than five hundred short stories, in almost every conceivable style. Some of the most interesting of his stories, most originally published in *Weird Tales*, are collected in *Far Lands and Other Days*.

Price retired from writing in 1952 and devoted himself to the study and practice of Buddhism. Twenty-seven years later he published his first fantasy novel, *The Devil Wives of Li Fong*. This is a Chinese fairy tale about a young man who marries two beautiful women who are actually serpent-demons. It is a charming story, written in the style of traditional Chinese wonder tales. This form and theme are seldom explored by Occidental writers, but are surprisingly well suited to the detached style and spare character development that marked Price's work in the early pulp years. (b. 1898)

RICHARD PURTILL makes fantasies set in the ancient Mediterranean world, when Minos ruled the sea and the unruly Olympians meddled constantly in the affairs (and affairs!) of humanity. Two novels, *The Golden Gryphon Feather* and *The Stolen Goddess*, are first-person narratives by young half-immortals, each of whom is caught up in the intrigues of Olympus and Earth.

The first, *The Golden Gryphon Feather*, is the story of Chryseis, an Athenian girl sent to Crete to join the sacred bull-dance. Through her friendship with Ariadne, she gradually comes to understand her heritage. *The Stolen Goddess* takes place many years later, after Crete has fallen to Theseus. The title refers to Persephone, who, contrary to popular belief, has eloped with Hades simply because she loves him.

These books are remarkable in that Purtill has created a magical world that is full of bright, dazzling light. Here are no misty enchantments, no twilight. The Olympians are tricky and not to be trifled with, but are essentially "human": loving, hating, and squabbling, just as the myths present them. The narrative style has a charming innocence that is well suited to the childhood of humankind. (b. 1931)

One of the most popular of the early contributors to *Weird Tales*, SEABURY QUINN had most impressive credentials for his work in the horror and supernatural genres. A lawyer, he taught mortuary law in New York for eight years and was for a time the editor of *Casket and Sunnyside*, a funeral directors' journal.

Quinn is best known for his short stories involving the detective Jules deGrandin. This sleuth is a cross between Sherlock Holmes and some sort of occult Hercule Poirot, and he and his assistant, Dr. Trowbridge, root out evil all over the world, but mostly in and around the fictional town of Harrisonville, New Jersey. This "local" setting was one thing that accounted for the popularity of these stories. The character of deGrandin was another plus for the series; a self-confident Frenchman with a high sense of morality and "higher law," he cows the police and the bad guys (or bad things) with his wit and humor, his keen intelligence, and his thick accent.

Not as well-known but at least as good are other short stories by Quinn. *Is the Devil a Gentleman?* is a collection put together by Quinn himself shortly before his death in 1969, and it contains a nicely ambiguous answer to the posed question, as well as two original and different views of werewolves, an adventurous and romantic time-travel fantasy, and several other excellent stories.

Roads is one of Quinn's few novels, and it has an interesting genesis. First requested from Quinn by a friend as a Christmas card and only later published by Arkham House as a book (with marvelous illustrations by Virgil Finlay), it's a retelling of an ancient Christian legend of Santa Claus. In this tale, Claus, a Norseman, was originally a gladiator in Jerusalem and retired to go home, but on his way he is responsible for saving a babe wrapped in swaddling clothes from Herod's soldiers. From this beginning we follow Claus through the death of Christ and the beginning of Christianity, and on through the ages to the start of gift-giving in celebration of Christmas. Other novels of Quinn's are *Alien Flesh*, based on Oriental magic, and *The Devil's Bride*, a tale starring Jules deGrandin and a Satanist plot. (1889–1969)

HUGH C. RAE. *Harkfast*, subtitled "The Making of a King," begins in the predawn mist of a fifth-century day with a raid by roving pirates on a small Pictish village. A young boy, lured away prior to the attack by strange lilting music, escapes, to be led by a deer to a small mountain valley populated by a band of Druids and a dying Celtic king. The boy, Ruan, has been chosen by the Druid Harkfast to replace the ruler.

The novel is the story of the search for an ancient talisman that will unite the scattered Celtic tribes under Ruan's rule. The magic here is, naturally, Druidic, of earth, sun, and moon, powerfully evoked by Mr. Rae.

The detail with which Rae describes the places and events, and the characterization provided by a first-rate writer, combine to make this novel seem so real that the reader is constantly tempted to check historical references to determine exactly when and where these events took place. (b. 1935)

In his brief career, TOM REAMY produced several short stories and one novel; most were science fiction, but all were written in such impeccable style, with so many haunting overtones of the fantastic, that readers of fantasy should not overlook any of them.

The short story "San Diego Light Foot Sue" is about an aging prostitute who falls in love with a young boy. Her despair at the situation leads her to magic, in search of some spell that will allow her to grow young again. This, and all of Reamy's stories, is written with searing realism that leaves the reader fully as shattered as the boy is by the result. The rest of Reamy's stories are collected with this one under the title *San Diego Light Foot Sue and Other Stories.*

The novel is called *Blind Voices* and is a stunning combination of period novel, fantasy, and s-f. During a Midwestern summer in the 1930s a circus comes to a small town. The exhibits are shocking; they include a minotaur, a harpy, a mermaid, and other mythological beasts, all quite real and all quite deadly. It is reminiscent of the circus in Peter Beagle's *The Last Unicorn*, but Reamy's almost tangible style brings the situation to life in all its gritty, horrid, and wonderful aspects. (1935–1977)

In 1967 and 1968 JOANNA RUSS wrote a brief series of sword-and-sorcery short stories; the stories are about Alyx, a rough-and-tumble independent woman. Alyx is, if not charming, then witty, passionate, light-fingered, and very good with a knife. She is a thief and a vagabond, and the world she inhabits is very like Fritz Leiber's Nehwon.

The stories are written with all of Russ's precision of language, and each is a nearly flawless example of short-story construction. Underneath each adventure lurks Russ's wicked sense of humor, just waiting for the opportunity to take a swipe at some cherished stereotype of sword-and-sorcery.

Alyx has grown and changed as Russ's career has grown.

life's energy was spent in composing and translating poetry. For another, his output in prose (almost all of it fantasy) was confined to short stories; all the books by Smith are collections of these. And for a third, most of these stories, over a hundred, were published in just seven years, from 1930 to 1936.

Dunsany was probably the greatest single influence on Smith's stories; they are elaborately exotic and more often than not set "beyond the fields we know," but they lack Dunsany's humor and irony, substituting instead a sense of evocative horror. Essentially, he stood somewhere just between the other two "Musketeers," placing Lovecraft's cosmic and larger-than-life (literally) terrors against Howard's created, glamorously remote settings.

Many of these settings were other planets, but remember, this was the era of "science fantasy," and locating a story on another planet or in the far future was about as technical as Smith ever got. The wonders in his stories are warlocks, magic, and strange beings.

The stories can be divided into several groups taking place more or less in the same locale, and have been collected at times in this way. There are the stories of "Hyperboria," of the remote past of Earth (and not to be confused with Howard's "Hyborian" stories, which, it has been suggested, were inspired by Smith's). Then there are the stories of Zothique, a continent of Earth's distant future; those of Poseidonis, "the last isle of foundering Atlantis"; and two and three stories laid respectively on the planets Xiccarph and Aihai (Mars.).

Smith's stories are rather lushly wrought (overwrought, according to his detractors) and extravagant in writing and concept, and it is suggested that they be taken a few at a time; they are much more effective that way. (1893–1961)

DAVID C. SMITH has written two novels based on characters created by Robert E. Howard and authorized by Howard's estate. The first is *The Witch of the Indies*; this is about Black Terence Vulmea, a pirate captain plying the waters of the West Indies, preying on Spanish galleons and British trade ships. Black Vulmea is caught up in a vengeful curse, cast upon him by a voodoo witch. The only person who can save him is Kate O'Donnell, pirate queen and even more powerful witch. This is wide-ranging sword-and-sorcery, with hard-drinking men and women risking their lives to uphold their own pirate code, and administering crude justice in a world where the mighty rule absolutely.

The second book is part of a series (by different authors) about Bran Mak Morn, another of Howard's characters. The title is *For the Witch of the Mists* (1978). Bran Mak Morn is a Pictish chieftain, fighting for his land against the Roman invaders. Battle is met with spells as often as with swords, as Bran cuts a wide swath through the Legions to the gates of Rome itself.

THORNE SMITH was a best-selling author in his day (the 1920s) but was forgotten to a degree, save for the films made from his works (some excellent, such as the Topper films and *I Married a Witch*). But nostalgia buffs will revel in his novels (they have a sort of literary art-deco feel to them in a curious way; they should all have covers depicting a lady sitting in a giant martini glass), and even those without a feeling for the Jazz Age could well find them great good fun (though, as Mae West might have said, goodness has nothing to do with them; they were considered rather naughty in the time when they were published).

They are all constructed in a generally similar way around a whimsical fantasy concept (given the opinion held until recently that the only way that the general public would accept fantasy was as whimsy) such as a swimming pool that is really the Fountain of Youth (*The Glorious Pool*), or a man who is a sort of werezoo and turns into any one of a variety of animals at unexpected times (*The Stray Lamb*), or a respectable financier haunted by a married couple of exceptionally raucous ghosts, not to mention their dog (*Topper*, of course).

Smith would throw this into a shaker, add liberal dashes of alcohol (his characters spent most of their time in various stages of inebriation) and suggestive situations (nothing graphic, though, despite the reputation for ribaldry) with a pinch of sophisticated cynicism. The results were a frothy cocktail with quite a kick for the reader.

Other variations Smith employed were the married couple suddenly transferred into each other's bodies in *Turnabout*, a hero with the habit of turning into a skeleton in *Skin and Bones*, and, in the wonderful *The Night Life of the Gods*, a gaggle of resuscitated Olympian deities set loose on an innocent New York City, with a particularly uproarious scene involving Neptune at the Fulton Fish Market.

Despite all the fun and games, though, Smith would sometimes throw a serious curve. For instance, *The Night Life of the Gods* comes to a downbeat and poignant conclusion.

It might be noted that few people know that Thorne Smith wrote one delightful fantasy for children, called *Lazy Bear Lane*. In it, an elderly couple are transformed into children and have wonderful adventures with a circus, a doll named Queen Elizabeth, and Lazy Bear himself, who "fairly bristles with magic."

Thorne Smith brought laughter and sophistication along with magic to the workaday world of his time; those qualities are still there in his writing for the lucky reader to find. (1892–1934)

NANCY SPRINGER has written a delightful, if somewhat derivative, fantasy-adventure series, beginning with *The White Hart* (1979) and continuing through *The Silver Sun* and *The Sable Moon*. The books are set in the land of Isle and are about its royal line, in whom the blood of gods and elves is mingled with mortal men.

The White Hart is the best book in the series, dealing as it does in pure myth. Beven is the child of a king and a goddess, raised with the fairy folk. His destiny calls him from the safety of his mother's realm, to answer a plea for help from a captive princess. Magic and intrigue surround Beven as he battles for the princess and the crown that is his birthright. A demigod to the end, Beven is unable to enjoy the fruits of his victories and must leave his kingdom in the hands of true mortals.

137

The Silver Sun (a rewrite of Springer's earlier *Book of Suns*) and *The Sable Moon* are both set much later in the history of Isle. These are less lyrical, more traditional fantasy novels, relying heavily on battle and the hero's native wit to further the plot. Springer handles the story well, drawing her characters so finely that the books are disappointing only when compared with *The White Hart*. The whole series is a very good read.

The ROBERT STALLMAN trilogy, the "Book of the Beast," rings a refreshing change on an old, old theme of horror-fantasy, the werebeast. Traditionally, the story is about a man who is changed into an animal, becoming a bestial horror; in Stallman's version the Beast is the true being, able to assume the appearance of a human, and forced by its own deep emotional needs to do so. The story, told in first person by the Beast and his various human personae, is set convincingly in the 1930s. *The Orphan* begins as the Beast first achieves consciousness. He learns to control his shape-changing ability and seeks desperately for the love and security of a human family that will take him in. The second book is called *The Captive*, and the third is *The Book of the Beast*. While the style of these books could be confusing (several "different" people telling a continuous story), Stallman handles the problem with remarkable skill, using the device to enhance both the tale and the Beast's bizarre but charming character.

It was a great loss to the world of fantasy when Robert Stallman died in 1980, shortly after completing the third book of this series. (1930–1980)

The writings of JAMES STEPHENS are steeped in Gaelic folklore and mythology. His best-known work is the novel *The Crock of Gold*, a most curious story with a cult following that transcends the readership of fantasy. It concerns two Philosophers, their wives, the Grey Woman of Dun Gortin and the Thin Woman of Inis Magrath, and their two children. Due to the theft of a washboard by the Leprecauns of Gort na Cloca Mora, the children are involved in a series of adventures that also include a crock of gold (of

course), the god Pan, and the police. Stephens has the legendary Irish gift of poetry, and the style of the novel is aphoristic, whimsical (though not cute), and ironically Dunsanian. The climax is a gathering of the Sluaige Shee, the Fairy Host of Ireland, to celebrate the wedding of Angus Og, the God of Love; it is breathtaking, and not only because of the loveliness of their names (Mananaan Mac Lir and his daughters Cliona and Aoife and Etain Fair-Hair, for instance).

The Crock of Gold is a delight as stylized as a piece of Celtic gold; it is hard to imagine anyone reading it and *not* becoming a member of its cult. (1882–1950)

Many writers have mined the gold in the legend of King Arthur, but MARY STEWART has done it in a very special way. Her books *The Crystal Cave, The Hollow Hills,* and *The Last Enchantment* are about that compelling, elusive figure, Merlin the Enchanter. She follows Merlin's life from his childhood all through his days of king-making and greatness, to his last, forgotten hour in the cave where he found his own destiny.

These books give a loving, detailed look at a world teetering on the brink of disaster—Rome is fallen, but the dream that was Rome lives on in its far-flung provinces. Merlin is of the older breed, a Briton, illegitimate child of a tribal chieftain's daughter and Ambrosius Aurelianus, last of the Roman generals. Merlin is also a seer, a man held in the hand of some god and driven by his foresight to create the future. Stewart has taken the legends of Merlin and the history of the times, and made of them an engrossing story of the age and the men that built the immortal court of Camelot. (b. 1916)

BRAM STOKER was an Irish theatrical manager at the turn of the century, a sometime playwright, and an extremely popular and gifted writer of horror stories. *The Jewel of the Seven Stars* is a chilling story about a woman who awakens after a long trancelike slumber; it is an effective variation on one of Poe's most often recurring themes. *The Lair of the White Worm* is a robust, exciting novel in

which earthly powers contend with each other in the guise of hawk, serpent, and dove, terrifying the residents of the ancient hills of Wessex. The short stories in *Dracula's Guest* (published posthumously) are finely crafted vignettes of horror, the sort that lurk in dreams long after the book is finished. Yet these stories have been eclipsed, almost lost, by the well-deserved reputation of Stoker's most famous novel, *Dracula*. Can there possibly be a person who has not heard of the infamous Count? Not seen the movie (*all* the movies), the cartoons, the *cereal boxes?* Well, perhaps not, but how many have read the book?

Dracula is an extraordinarily powerful novel about the encounter between an ancient evil (the vampire) and the vigorous modernity of the nineteenth century; between the passionate sensualist and the chill inflexibility of reason. Stoker dressed all this up with Gothic ruins and superstitious peasants, garlic, bats, and nonreflecting mirrors. He created a monster, and did it perhaps too well; the enduring success of Dracula (the character, as opposed to the novel), rests not on the strength and skill with which those noble young men and Dr. Van Helsing resist the vampire, but on Stoker's compelling portrayal of the fatal attractiveness of evil. The tables have turned, and today it is the Count who is the hero, and Van Helsing the villain.

Dracula is a masterpiece of gothic horror, the wellspring from which all the other interpretations rise. Stoker's creation stalks through modern horror as he once did the streets of London, changing shape as often as necessary, and never, never dying. (1847–1912)

PETER STRAUB slipped slowly into the fantasy/horror genre novel by novel. His first book was a mainstream work and his second a Henry Jamesian (is the ghost in the attic or the mind?) novel, and then he decided that it was cheating not to reveal the ghost, so he wrote *If You Could See Me Now*. His popularity began to rise with *Ghost Story*, an extremely literate and logical novel with elements of nightmare and fantasy. The characters and the small town in which the action takes place are particularly well drawn, and the atmosphere and structure of the novel add

140

to the tale's effect. *Shadowland* should probably be considered fantasy rather than horror, if there is a true distinction; it's a study of magic, its potential, and the use and abuse of its power. As in *Ghost Story*, the structure, at first a little confusing, and the atmosphere, very discomforting, heighten the impact on the reader. (b. 1943)

To read a story by THEODORE STURGEON is to meet characters you care about, characters that you love or hate, that you understand intimately or just can't get a grasp on. To read a work of fantasy by Sturgeon is to meet these people slipped or thrown into a situation where logic doesn't work, where heart and soul matter more than thought and reason.

Sturgeon's fantasy is restricted to short stories, his novels being of other genres, and ranges from humor to horror, touching almost every base between. There is "Bianca's Hands," a quiet story about a very ugly girl with very beautiful hands—or maybe it's about a very beautiful pair of hands with an ugly girl attached. "It" is a living thing that was never born, an amalgam of all that's vile and frightening. And then there's "The Professor's Teddy Bear," a child's toy that doesn't play around. In another vein, "The Silken Swift" is almost pure high fantasy, instructions in the care and loving of a unicorn, and "The Graveyard Reader" tells a lovely tale of tombstones. In "Shadow, Shadow on the Wall" the shadow knows, and acts, and in "Shottle Bop" blind justice does the same, with a little help from the Other World. "Ghost of a Chance" demonstrates Sturgeon's sense of humor in a story of a jealous ghost and a lovesick human.

Sturgeon's works in this genre are scattered among his collections, but a few have a higher percentage, *E Pluribus Unicorn* and *Not without Sorcery* being particularly fantasy-laden. Search through his writings—whether fantasy, science fiction, or whatever, it's good stuff to read. (b. 1918)

It can be flatly stated that the works of THOMAS BURNETT SWANN are unique. No one has ever written anything like his odd mixtures of fantasy and history, light as soap bubbles but also permeated with an elegant sexuality. He himself described his work as "domestic rather than epic fantasies," and while "domestic" seems an odd word to apply to his characters, often amoral or ribald mythological creatures and heros, Swann did work small, concentrating on wistful wispy emotions and situations rather than grand passions and adventures.

Certainly some of the major attractions of Swann's stories are the surprising characterizations that he gives beings such as dryads, minotaurs, and fauns. In his hands they are not frightening forces of nature or half-divine demigods; they are almost always very human, or in some cases subhuman, flawed by their very lack of humanity and touching in their simplicity.

Swann's uses of history and myth are also highly individual. He makes no pretense of historical veracity; he is essentially writing his own mythology, sometimes using the stuff of older legend, sometimes creating it as he goes, sometimes giving us rather startling juxtapositions as in *How Are the Mighty Fallen*. Set in ancient Palestine, it purports to be the story of David and Jonathan (with some ideas about their emotional involvement that might surprise biblical scholars), but also manages to work in sirens, cyclopes, and a dryad or two. *The Minikins of Yam* is set in the Old Kingdom of Egypt, and is based on a real letter from the young Pharaoh, Pepy II, asking for a dancing dwarf from the land of Yam; Swann's fantasy variation on this historical theme is typically unexpected.

Lady of the Bees takes us to early Italy and the story of Romulus and Remus, while in *The Not-World*, it is eighteenth-century England, with some odd survivals from the Celtic past. *The Forest of Forever* tells of the last minotaur, and *Green Phoenix* depicts Aeneas after Troy falls as well as the dryad who will later be on hand for the founding of Rome in *Lady of the Bees* (dryads and bees are Swann's most persisent themes).

Moondust is set at the siege of Jericho, *The Weirwoods* in ancient Etruria, *Day of the Minotaur* in Knossos. As is obvious from this flood of titles, Swann was prolific in a relatively short writing career, luckily for those who acquired a taste for his odd and interesting little "domestic" fantasies. (1928–1976)

The name of W. W. TARN (a.k.a. Sir William Woodthorpe Tarn) has not been remembered; it would be nice to say that the one fantasy credited to him has been, but that also has been long lost to readers. This is unfortunate, because it is a small jewel. Its title is *The Treasure of the Isle of Mist*, and the book was first published just after World War I. The Isle of Mist is one of the fiercely beautiful islands off the coast of Scotland. On it live young Fiona and her father, the Scholar.

Fiona is promised the quest for the treasure of the Isle of Mist by the mysterious peddler who appears over the moors with his little black dog. They appear in many guises throughout the story; their real identity is one of many surprises of the quest. Among the others are an interview with a centipede ("Congratulations," said the centipede. "We *are* getting on. You wanted badly to shudder and you didn't."), a hunt for the King of the Woodcock, a poignant encounter with the Oread spirit of the mountain Heleval, and a perilous trip to the fairy-world to confront a convocation of the Good Folk of many lands to rescue her friend, the Urchin.

The story is told with the wonderful Gaelic talent for combining cleverness, poetry, and wit, reminiscent of Stephens's *The Crock of Gold*. And a word must be said for the illustrations by Robert Lawson for a later American edition; they are among the most beautiful of that extraordinary artist's drawings. (1869–1957)

RUTH PLUMLY THOMPSON was privileged as few people are. When she was barely twenty, she was chosen to continue a favorite and famous fantasy series after the death of its original author. The series was the renowned Oz books, and she did very well indeed by the assignment, writing one a year for nineteen years. Her Oz books were lighter in tone than Baum's, with less of the darker elements that he sometimes used, and endlessly inventive in new characters and places to be found in the beloved fairyland. She was also inventive with language, making frequent use of puns both dreadful and wonderful. (1900–1976)

A man of many words was JAMES THURBER, and most of them funny. He wrote and cartooned for *The New Yorker*, did reviews and character sketches for other magazines, had plays produced on Broadway and translated to film, and he wrote several short fantasies.

What stands out most in Thurber's work is his warm, witty, wacky, and wonderful way with words. (He goes in big for alliteration, onomatopoeia, and such.) As an example, this short section of *The Thirteen Clocks*:

The brambles and thorns grew thick and thicker in a ticking thicket of bickering crickets. Farther along and stronger, bonged the gongs of a throng of frogs, green and vivid on their lily pads. From the sky came the crying of flies and the pilgrims leaped over a bleating sheep creeping knee-deep in a sleepy stream. . . .

And it goes on like this. This particular story is about a princess in distress, a prince in disguise, a quest, and all the other good things fairy tales are made of, and, best of all, it's about eighty-five pages of Thurber at play.

The White Deer is the story of a beautiful girl who's a deer, or a deer who's a dear, or a dear girl. Again there's a quest, complete with wizards and dwarfs, perilous pursuit, and an ending as touching and romantic as could be asked. (As an added bonus, this book is illustrated by the author.)

Wordplay turns to letterplay in *The Wonderful O*. Two villains searching a tropical island for treasure are thwarted, and seek their revenge on the islanders by taking over and banning all words containing the letter O. The reader is truly amazed at the number of words that need that letter, including "valour," "hope," and "love," and one other that is possibly even more important.

Among Thurber's shortest works are "Many Moons," about a princess who asks the impossible, the king's advisers who are stumped at the request, and the court jester who comes up with the answer, and two collections of fables for our times, entitled *Fables for Our Times* and *Further Fables for Our Times*, most of which originally appeared in *The New Yorker*.

Almost all of Thurber's work is "serious," in the sense that he comments on the human condition, but is leavened with such high humor that the moral doesn't get at all in the way of the enjoyment, even in the fables, where the moral is printed at the end of the story. (1894–1961)

The name J. R. R. TOLKIEN is known to millions. His books are probably the most famous and widely read fantasies in history. Of all the Inklings (see LEWIS for more on the Inklings), he was the most successful—and paradoxically, the least successful, since his popular reputation rests on the enchanting adventure of his *The Lord of the Rings*, not on the mystical and religious values expressed in *The Silmarillion*, over which he labored for nearly thirty years.

Tolkien's created world of Middle-Earth, like Lewis's Narnia, was begun as a parable, a way for the writer to convey his own very deep spiritual beliefs to others; the first section of *The Silmarillion*, "The Ainulindale," is a clear statement of how Tolkien saw the underlying truth of the universe. But the elaborate, multifaceted world of Middle-Earth, and the epic of heroic fantasy which animates it, ultimately overshadowed the earlier, more profound work.

In reality, all of the books set in Middle-Earth, *The Silmarillion*, *The Hobbit*, and the three books of *The Lord of the Rings*, form a single tale with some parts more extensively told than others. It grew out of Tolkien's love of words, his intimate knowledge of north-European mythology, and stories he told to his son.

For those who have not yet encountered Professor Tolkien's creation, Middle-Earth is a world wherein dwell Elves, Dwarves, Ents, Men, and Hobbits; beings whose destinies are guided by the Valar, the Powers who govern the world. They are opposed by the Enemy, a fallen Vala; his servant Sauron; and a host of Orcs, Trolls, dragons, and evil Men.

145

The story of *The Lord of the Rings* is a quest: one Hobbit takes it upon himself (although it is his destiny) to carry the One Ring, a mighty sorcerous weapon, into the heart of Sauron's realm, the only place where it can be destroyed.

The Hobbit, an earlier book in the story, was written for children, and tells of the adventures of a Hobbit and the finding of the Ring. *The Silmarillion*, first written but last published, is in effect the Bible of Middle-Earth. It presents the Creation and the long early ages of Middle-Earth, all in spare, mythic prose which only hints at the great joys and sorrows, defeats and victories that occurred before the end of the tale in the trilogy.

The beauty and wonder of Middle-Earth is its complexity—the reader is provided with several different languages, alphabets, genealogies, geographies, and histories, complete and consistent down to the smallest detail. Tolkien's prose is magnificently descriptive, whether he is describing a battle between wizards or how it feels to fall down in a swamp. This, indeed, is why the books are so compulsively rereadable—there are so many gems of imagery that no one can catch them all in a single reading.

In addition to the Middle-Earth stories, Tolkien wrote several short fairy tales. *Leaf by Niggle* is an allegory, although that word has certain negative connotations that should not be applied to this story. It is about the value of being a dreamer in a world of practicalities, and the rewards of being true to one's own inner vision. This story is generally published with an essay by Tolkien, "On Fairy-stories"; originally an Andrew Lang lecture, it was first published in a small book, *Essays Presented to Charles Williams*, as a tribute to his friend. "On Fairy-stories" is one of the finest statements about the history, nature, and value of the fairy tale ever made; it illuminates Tolkien's own writings and, if needed, will provide a more than acceptable public justification for the secret and childlike delight in fairy tales that many adults cherish.

Farmer Giles of Ham is the adventures (or misadventures) of a country man who became a king. It is a delightful tale full of dragons, knights, crafty kings, and brave animals; in the end it is true courage and down-to-earth common sense that win the day.

Smith of Wootton Major is a more delicate sort of story, about the interweaving of the world of Faerie and the world of mortal men. In a village out of time, one child is given a token, and with the token the ability to enter Faerie. The gift passes in secret from the previous bearer to the newly chosen one; families are drawn closer together as a glimmer of enchantment slowly spreads over the entire town.

Despite his rich legacy of fantasy to the world, Tolkien's vocation was not as a novelist. He was a scholar of languages, primarily Anglo-Saxon and Old English; his wonderful, acclaimed translations of the literature of those times are the professional standards. The most generally available are his *Beowulf* and, published in a single volume, *Sir Gawain and the Green Knight*, *Pearl*, and *Sir Orfeo*. Although these works have often been diminished to curiosities of antiquity, they remain magnificent fantasies, and Tolkien brought his own love of Faerie to the translations. He thus brought them back from the realm of scholars to lovers of the fantastic in modern times. (1892–1973)

Those who know P. L. TRAVERS's acerbic creation, Mary Poppins, only through the persona of Julie Andrews, do not really know Mary Poppins, despite the best efforts of that charming actress. Mary Poppins seldom has a kind word for anyone, almost never smiles except at her own prim reflection, and can get four children washed and in bed with No Nonsense Whatsoever.

But the lucky Banks children who find themselves in the charge of this jewel of nursemaids do seem to find themselves encountering the most amazing adventures. Some are hilarious, such as a visit with Mary's Uncle Albert Wigg, who becomes filled with laughing gas if his birthday falls on a Friday and tends to float near the ceiling. Some can be terrifying, as when Jane enters the picture on a Royal Doulton china bowl, and almost becomes trapped in the past by some sinister Victorian children. And some are cosmic: a Circus of the Constellations on Mary's night out, or a wild New Year's party that takes place in "the Crack," that time between the first stroke of midnight and the last, when it is neither the old year nor the new.

There's a great deal of J. M. Barrie's whimsy in the Mary Poppins stories, but they are saved from stickiness by Mary's acid character and the touches of poetry and hints of grander, stranger magic that lie behind many of the adventures. (b. 1906)

Kane, cursed with immortality and doomed to wander eternally, is the creation of KARL EDWARD WAGNER and is one of the most popular of the literary descendants of Conan. He is also one of the brightest, there being a gleam of intelligence and humor in his eyes along with the obligatory blood lust. Not that there's not blood enough; each of Kane's adventures has a body count that will satisfy and which usually includes the mortal remains of some creature of the supernatural—the land which Kane wanders has werewolves, vampires, and ghouls aplenty, as well as ogres and sorcerers (and "esses"), not to mention vicious humans. Wagner's writing is primarily responsible for Kane's popularity; characterization is emphasized—the reader slowly gets to know the protagonist through several short stories and novels, and Wagner doesn't stint on the secondary characters—enemies and allies, natural and supernatural, are well drawn, and the land itself, usually harsh and bitter, is atmospherically described.

Wagner has also done some work with two of the characters created by Robert E. Howard. *Legion from the Shadows* stars Bran Mak Morn, and Wagner is author of one of the "new" Conan novels. For those who enjoy the mayhem-and-magic school of fantasy, Wagner is one of the best. (b. 1945)

Fantasy role-playing games are becoming extremely popular, and HUGH WALKER's novels are an outgrowth of that popularity. In 1967, in Sweden, Walker and some friends created the world of Magira, where sword-and-sorcery rule the land, damsels and kingdoms are in regular distress, and where the acts of the gods are based on a roll of the dice. The "Magira" series is made up of "historical novels"—the history being that of the game over its years of play.

From the fascinating premise of one of the players being drawn physically into Magira, Walker carries the reader through several well-written novels of adventure and magic, and in the process gives the nongamer a look into the world of fantasy games.

EVANGELINE WALTON is best known for her delightful retelling of the Mabinogion, that ancient Welsh myth cycle that is the wellspring of so much modern fantasy. Walton brought to the Mabinogion the novelist's gift of filling in a spare account of events with conversation, motivation, and vivid description, yet retaining the elusive otherworldliness of the original. True not only to the spirit but the shape of the original, Walton wrote four books, one for each "branch" of the Mabinogion.

The first is *The Prince of Annwm*; it tells of Prince Pwyll of Dyved and his bargain with Arawn, king of the underworld. The second branch is *The Children of Llyr*. It is the story of the mighty heroes who became gods: Bran, the king; Manawyddan his wise brother; Nissyen and Evnissyn, twins begotten on their mother as an act of vengeance; and Branwen, the white lady of Britain, whose wrongs brought devastation to Ireland. Third is *The Song of Rhiannon*, a tale of the wanderings of Manawyddan and Rhiannon. Last is *The Island of the Mighty*, perhaps the most familiar branch. It tells of Math, Son of Mathonwy, King of Gwynedd; his heir Gwydion and his niece Arianrhod; and the fostering and betrayal of Arianrhod's son, Llew Llaw Gyffes.

The Mabinogion itself exists in many fine translations, and Walton's adaptations should not be read as a substitute—she infused it with much of her own thoughts and attitudes about power and honor, making her version of the epic a personal statement about its relevance to our own time. (b. 1907)

One of the most popular writers for the famous pulp, *Weird Tales*, MANLY WADE WELLMAN is also one of those who continue to write. Very prolific, Wellman has written over sixty-five novels and several hundred short stories, most of the novels being either science fiction, mainstream, or nonfiction. (He was nominated for the Pulitzer Prize for one of his Southern histories.)

His knowledge of the South and its ways, particularly of the southern Appalachian mountains, form the basis for the stories about his best-known character, Silver John or John the Balladeer. John is a minstrel who wanders through the mountains with a silver-stringed guitar on his back, and who seems to have a phenomenal affinity for all that is strange and supernatural in his area. Told in first person, and in very strong mountain dialect, these stories read as if John is sitting by the potbellied stove in the general store, talking to the good ol' boys, maybe once in a while pausing to dip into the cracker or pickle barrel. John's a good fellow, and high intelligence and common sense shine through the down-home talk. Most of his appearances are in short stories, and all but a few of these are collected in *Who Fears the Devil*, but there are novels as well. *The Old Gods Waken* is the first, and John finds himself fighting a strange combination of Druidic and American Indian magic. This is followed by *After Dark*.

Wellman's contribution to the fantasy genre is by no means limited to the Silver John stories. Collected in *Worse Things Waiting* are twenty-seven short stories, two novelettes, and a poem. Two of the short stories are early adventures of John, but the others range from a Lovecraftian salute, "The Terrible Parchment," through confrontations with well-known creatures such as kelpies ("The Kelpie") and vampires ("The Devil Is Not Mocked"), to tales of people who are just plain strange, such as "The Undead Soldier." The two novelettes take place in just-post-Civil-War South and star Sergeant "Bible" Jaeger, ex-soldier and now-preacher, who has things more evil than bingo cheats to fight.

Wellman is a writer as good as he is prolific, and his output is so varied that anyone interested in the fiction of the supernatural is sure to find something enjoyable. (b. 1905)

Much of the science fiction of H. G. WELLS was "meaningful," and this applies to his fantasy as well, but the fantasy is a lot funnier. *The Sea Lady* is a mermaid who is saved from drowning (as we all know, a mermaid doesn't drown —she knew perfectly well what she was doing) by a young British aristocrat. Her views of his stuffy life style and his beginning realization of the freedom of hers make for both the meaning and the humor in this one. *The Wonderful Visit* has many of the same elements but is much more poignant. It's the story of an angel fallen to Earth who begins to become human and to fall in love with a human woman.

Some of Wells's short fiction is in the fantasy vein, best known being "The Man Who Could Work Miracles," about a quiet little clerk who is endowed by the gods with the power to do, literally, anything he wishes.

Whether or not you are one for the message of the medium, Wells's humor and wit make his works thoroughly enjoyable if only for the fun of it. (1866–1946)

Using as the basis for a fantasy a religion that is practiced in the present day is difficult, but ROBERT WESTALL manages to do it without coming off like a revival meeting.

The Wind Eye takes place at and around a cottage far up the Northumbrian coast of England, in the mid-1970s— and in the far past. Using Church records and legends about St. Cuthbert and time travel, Westall fashions an exciting tale of Vikings and demons and rescues and religion. Catholicism also plays a small part in *The Watch House*, a chilling ghost story that goes into the possible reasons for and characters of ghosts in general, and two in specific.

Time-shifting figures strongly in *The Devil on the Road*, as does magic, both black and white—and possibly shades of gray. A rambunctious young Englishman stops at a deserted barn for the night while on a motorcycle vacation. There a strange, wild cat that mysteriously appears and disappears, the reaction of the owner of the barn to John Webster's presence there, and the way the people of the nearby village start bringing him little presents and calling him "Cunning," are part of the puzzle whose pieces also include an interesting look at witchcraft in English history.

Most of Westall's protagonists are young, in their teens; the darkness of his themes, his ability to create character and atmosphere, and his attention to historical detail all recommend him to an adult reader. (b. 1929)

Atypically for a writer of fantasy, T. H. WHITE was the author of a best-seller (not to mention the basis for a hit Broadway musical and a major motion picture). It was, of course, *The Once and Future King* (which Lerner and Loewe distorted into *Camelot*), that charming, funny, tragic look at the life of King Arthur.

Perhaps somewhere in the world there is someone who doesn't know about this book, in which case it should be noted that it tells of the boyhood of Arthur, fostered in the castle of the good Sir Ector; Arthur's ascension to the throne and the creation of the Round Table; his love for Guenever and Lancelot and its unhappy outcome; and the final dissolution of Camelot by the machinations of Morgan and Mordred, Arthur's son by Morgan's sister.

It is how this familiar story is told that makes *The Once and Future King* so special. White recounts it in an unbuttoned, informal, slangy style that makes it terribly modern; the magic of the period is taken totally for granted; and the often hilarious humor is due primarily to a skillful use of anachronism, generally provided by Merlyn (for instance, his set of the fourteenth edition of the *Encyclopaedia Britannica*, "marred as it was by the sensationalism of the popular plates"), who lives backward in time. This means he knows the future, but has a terrible time sorting out what *has* happened to everyone else.

What many readers do not know is that the first three sections of *The Once and Future King* (respectively, "The Sword in the Stone," "The Queen of Air and Darkness," and "The Ill-Made Knight") were published earlier as individual novels[2] and had been extensively rewritten for the omnibus volume, which also included a final, heretofore

---

[2] The second part was originally titled *The Witch in the Wood*.

unpublished section, "The Candle in the Wind." Many who have read the earlier versions prefer them, since several marvelous scenes have been omitted entirely. Not easily forgotten are Arthur's visit to the castle of Morgan Le Fay, a stronghold full of goodies like chocolates, sodas, and other things that hadn't been invented yet (a wonderful twist on Hansel and Gretel's witch's house), and the skating carnival organized by Queen Morgause of the Orkneys.

After White's death, *The Book of Merlyn,* called "the unpublished last chapter of *The Once and Future King,*" finally appeared.

For those who know only White's Arthurian stories, there are several other treats in store. In *Mistress Masham's Repose,* young Maria discovers a colony of Lilliputians, descended from a group that Gulliver had brought back, unrecorded by Swift. Maria is an impoverished orphan, under the care of a wicked vicar and an even wickeder governess. She is the heiress to the enormous estate of Malplaquet, "about four times longer than Buckingham Palace, but falling down . . . it was surrounded by Vistas, Obelisks, Pyramids, Columns, Temples, Rotundas, and Palladian Bridges." Anyone who has been to England's Blenheim Palace, home of the Churchills, will know where White got his inspiration for Malplaquet.

Maria becomes the Lilliputians' friend and protectress, but horrors! her wicked guardians find out about the little people and want to capture them and show them to the public for a lot of money.

The rest of the plot is devoted to how Maria prevents this, with the help of faithful Cook ("Rule Britannia is my motter"), her old dog Captain ("It is uncanny how canine a human can be if you are kind to them"), and the most absentminded professor of all time. It's all absolutely hilarious, but underneath, White is making the kind of moral truths and psychological insights that he did in the Arthurian series.

And there are also *The Elephant and the Kangaroo,* in which White does for Noah's ark what he did for Arthur, and *The Master,* a slight but exciting tale of how two children foil an archcriminal who is out to rule the world.

T. H. White occupies a special place in the world of fan-

153

tasy. It would certainly be difficult to name another author in that field who is so universally loved, except perhaps Tolkien. (1906–1964)

LEONARD WIBBERLY is best known to fantasy readers for his series of books about the tiny Duchy of Grand Fenwick, five miles long and three miles wide, located in the mountainous regions of eastern France. Grand Fenwick was ceded by the French to a tiny band of English longbowmen in 1475, and their descendants have held it to the present day. The first in the series is *Beware of the Mouse*, which tells the story of the founders of the Duchy. The next, and probably the most famous, is *The Mouse That Roared*. In it, the advisers of the Grand Duchess Gloriana recommend that Grand Fenwick declare war on the United States, in order to lose. In this way they will receive foreign aid for reconstruction, and that will allow Grand Fenwick to get out of debt. There is just one hitch—the army of Grand Fenwick (a handful of longbowmen) can't seem to lose. In fact, they win the war. Third is *The Mouse on the Moon*. A freak accident shows that the premier vintage of Grand Fenwick and its primary export, Pinot Grand Fenwick, is actually an incredibly powerful rocket fuel. In its never-ending quest for money, Grand Fenwick launches an expedition to the moon. Finally, there is *The Mouse on Wall Street*. Suddenly Grand Fenwick has too much money, and it is ruining everyone's life. In desperation the government decides to speculate on Wall Street, assured that this is a sure way to lose millions of dollars. Typically, matters get out of hand—it seems that the prestige of Grand Fenwick is so high that they can't lose a dime.

The Mouse books are, to use a tired adjective, rollicking fun. To read them is to chuckle, laugh, gasp, and groan as the events hurtle on to an inevitable, impossible conclusion. Wibberly is a master of incongruous humor, and his books are rare examples of really funny fantasy. (b. 1915)

OSCAR WILDE is often first thought of as a playwright. Then one remembers *The Picture of Dorian Gray*, that strange novel that is a combination of fantasy, horror, and mystery. More search into his output also reveals his fairy tales, most of which are collected in *The Happy Prince and Other Stories*.

Dorian Gray, though a story of a man's attempt to familiarize himself with every sort of decadence and evil, reads as a delightfully witty and at times humorous novel, to modern eyes. The decadence seems not so decadent and the evil not so evil to us, and Wildean epigrams sprinkle the pages.

The hard edge of Wilde's wit is softened in his fairy tales and mellowed by a gentle humor and the love for his children, for whom these stories were written. There is "The Happy Prince," a glittering golden statue in the village square, who, with the help of a swallow constantly trying to leave for Egypt, brings happiness to the less-fortunate in the town. Another is "The Selfish Giant," whose garden is constantly in the grip of winter until he shows love for a small child. These are warm stories, possibly a bit moralistic for some tastes, but a joy especially to those who like "children's stories." (1854–1900)

CHARLES WILLIAMS was perhaps the most mystical and least overtly Christian of the Inklings. (See LEWIS for more on the Inklings.) In his books he demonstrates a deep knowledge and understanding of traditional magical theories and implements, and invests them all with power as symbols of an absolute reality which underlies the manifest reality of the visible world. Unlike Lewis and Tolkien, Williams did not create a magical world; in his novels he set the Powers at work in contemporary England. In each book a different aspect of Power comes into the hands of very ordinary people, who must choose by their actions the fate of, if not the world, their own souls.

All this may sound dry as dust and as hard to swallow, but it isn't. Williams cast it all into delightful, occasionally madcap form. In *Many Dimensions*, the Seal of Solomon (with the power to instantly transport a person to any place on Earth) falls into the hands of an up-and-coming capitalist who plans to corner the transportation industry with it. *War in Heaven*, a quest for the Grail, is a bizarre murder mystery—and the Grail is found in a small village with the unlikely name of Fardles. One of Williams's most memorable characters is Sybil in *The Greater Trumps*; when the forces of nature are accidentally set free, she wanders about in a hurricane-force snowstorm calmly collecting her family and protecting a kitten.

It is Williams's powers of characterization, more than anything else, that make his books so engrossing. He makes it very clear that no one is entirely good or entirely evil, and that each person must consciously choose to be primarily one or the other. Each actor in the story is drawn with such detail that the reader can identify fully with him when the character is brought face to face with spiritual truths.

Williams wrote a total of seven novels; the other titles are *The Place of the Lion, Descent Into Hell, Shadows of Ecstasy*, and *All Hallows' Eve*. (1886–1945)

AUSTIN TAPPAN WRIGHT is known essentially for only one book. but what a book! There is nothing like the towering novel *Islandia* in all of literature.

> The country of Islandia forms the southern and temperate portion of the Karain subcontinent, which lies in the Southern Hemisphere. It is inhabited by a white race, ancient in history, agricultural in civilization. To this country in 1908 the young American, John Lang, goes as the first American consul, to discover a world that is alien yet compelling, traditional yet free, strange yet totally plausible. . . .

says Sylvia Wright in the Introduction to *Islandia*.

In the two years that Lang spends in Islandia, we slowly get to know—through his eyes—her culture, people, and countryside. It is during that period that the Islandian council is debating the wisdom of opening Islandia to the dubious advantages of foreign trade, influence, and (potential) exploitation. The decision is negative, and all foreigners are to be expelled. However, Lang, due to an extraordinary circumstance which he would be the last to call heroic, is invited to stay.

He decides to return to the U.S. for a year to give his own culture a chance. After doing so, he opts for Islandia, asking an American girl to join him there as his wife. She does so, and he struggles to help her make the adaptation to an alien way of life as he has done—with eventual success.

This is all that "happens" in *Islandia*, but this unique and extraordinary novel is so rich, so full, and so monumental in concept that no real appraisal of the values to be found in its nearly one thousand pages is possible.

One question to answer before even making the attempt: is *Islandia* a fantasy, since it is totally realistic in style and has no supernatural (in the literal sense of the word) events whatsoever? A difficult question to answer; the issue must be begged by saying that *Islandia* is certainly speculative. It hypothesizes not a created world, but something more difficult—a created nation and culture interacting with historical and geographical realities.

It is not just a travelogue through a Utopic wonderland, though. There is drama in the novel, some of it intensely personal, some adventurous. There is a great amount of what could be called philosophy, particularly in an extensive evaluation of Western culture. But the major *raison d'être* of *Islandia* is Islandia. It is tempting to throw out a potpourri of fragments of Islandia's culture, but it is so completely and organically conceived that it would be like trying to convey the totality of Japan by mentioning the *obi* and the custom of hara-kiri.

It must suffice to say that the numerous Islandian characters are varied and idiosyncratic, but all reflect the Islandian culture, which in turn reflects the historical and geographical circumstances of the country. However, it is irresistible to cite examples of the Islandian names and language; they are as successful and *right* as those of Tolkien, but so very different. Islata Soma, Morana, Stellin and Stellina, Hytha Nattana, Inerria, Winder, Doringclorn, Earne, the Islar are Islandian place and people names and titles. And in the language, for example, the several words for love—*ania, apia, alia*—indicate a very real semantic reflection of a uniquely Islandian concept.

Yet this creation of an entire culture is not all the book has to offer. John Lang is by contemporary standards an inhibited, turn-of-the-century prude; yet in his intelligent but often troubled approach to the conflicts between Islandian and American mores, we learn more about pre-World War I America than any memoir of the time could tell us. And by extension, as we watch the sophisticated Islandians, viewed as "primitive" by the Westerners because they resist technology, maneuver to keep their integrity ("the right of a nation to be individualistic," as Lang puts it), we see the methods that Europe and America used to coax and bully other nations into commercial dependency and exploitability.

One of the most startling aspects of *Islandia* is its accurate anticipation of the current trend toward the "natural" and the unspoiled and against the unbridled spread of technology and commercialism. The extremely critical, though not vindictive, view of Western civilization as guided by these principles, directly stated by Wright through his narrator and indirectly but even more powerfully shown by contrast with the Islandia culture, makes it a thoroughly modern document. (It was first published in 1942, after many years in conception and realization.)

Austin Tappan Wright's *Islandia* is one of the great achievements of speculative creation. Norman Cousins perhaps put it best and most succinctly: he called *Islandia* "a miracle."

Some further notes on *Islandia*: the word Islandia itself is pronounced by giving *island* its English pronunciation, and with the emphasis on "land." There is a sequel, *The Islar*, written by Wright's friend, Mark Saxton; it takes place just after World War II and is a fairly conventional Cold War thriller, but an interesting footnote to Islandian history for Islandiophiles. (1883-1931)

CHELSEA QUINN YARBRO is many things: composer, mystery writer, occultist, historian, and fantasist. In her works of fantasy she combines the discipline of scholarship and the evocative gift of the storyteller; not since Mary Renault has a writer brought such historical veracity to fiction.

Yarbro is best known for her series of vampire books—

based, for a change, not on Dracula but on Le Comte de Saint-Germain. Saint-Germain is an historical personage who appeared in Paris in the mid-eighteenth century and provoked a flurry of rumor and speculation. The man claimed to be an immortal alchemist. What is known is that he was immensely wealthy and talented. He wrote poetry and music and spoke at least twelve languages. He always wore either black or white, never appeared during the day, and was never seen to eat or drink. All these facts and more are attested to by letters and articles written at the time by reputable people, whose only interest was curiosity about this enigmatic man. Yarbro's answer to the speculation about Saint-Germain is that he was (is) an immortal vampire. In a series of books, she is tracing his career back through time, deftly inserting the Count into history. The first book is *Hotel Transylvania*, where Saint-Germain becomes involved with a group of really frightening satanists in Paris in 1743. The second book, *The Palace*, sees Francesco Ragoczy da San Germano in Renaissance Florence, confronting the zealous ascetic Savonarola in the court of Lorenzo de' Medici. *Blood Games* is third, and is set in Nero's Rome. Here Ragoczy Sanct' Germain Franciscus is swept up in the final debauched years of Nero's rule.

In these books Yarbro is doing a remarkable thing—she began in *Hotel Transylvania* with a very urbane and humane vampire, and as the books move back in time she is showing how he became that way. These books are not for the squeamish—Yarbro doesn't pull her punches. With each appearance the Count is slightly more cruel, a little less human. With more than three thousand years to trace, she has room for several more novels; the final book with the Count as a savage, almost bestial, new-made vampire should be something to see.

Ariosto is fantasy in a different vein; this is a delicate, complex novel that balances two fantasy worlds. The first, which Yarbro calls *La Realta*, is an alternate renaissance where Ludovico Ariosto (himself an historical figure) becomes involved in the Medici intrigues against Henry VIII of England. The second, *La Fantasia*, is Ariosto's own novel about an Italian-dominated American Empire, with himself as hero. The two parts balance each other, as

Ariosto's actions in each world are affected by the events in the other. *Ariosto* is not an easy book; it doesn't sweep the reader away into thundering adventure. It is, however, a peculiarly satisfying manipulation of reality. (b. 1942)

There is a fine line, which probably need not be drawn, between the science fiction and the fantasy of ROGER ZELAZNY. *Isle of the Dead* seems to begin as the former, taking place in the future, with spaceships zooming around and alien world-shaping techniques forming a great part of the plot, but it soon becomes clear that the planetscaping powers of protagonist Francis Shandow are inextricably linked with the alien god Shimbo of Darktree. When one of Shimbo's enemies among the alien pantheon "animates" another human, there is a smash-bang *götterdämmerung* for two. *Jack of Shadows* has a middle that may be construed as science fiction of a very strange sort, but the beginning and the end are definitely fantasy. This novel takes place in the far future or the long past of a world which could be Earth, but which doesn't turn on its axis, leaving one side in perpetual dark while the other is light. And there is the band of shadow between the two, realm of Jack of Shadows or Shadowjack, a sorcerer on the dark, or magic, side of this world. Seeking revenge on some Darksiders for transgressions against his person (they have him executed, and he is forced to undergo a painful physical and psychic ordeal in order to reincarnate), Jack travels to the light side, land of reason and logic. There he learns cybernetics, which he combines with his own powers to bring about the denouement.

   Zelazny's major work in the fantasy field, at least in length, is the "Amber Quintet": *Nine Princes in Amber*, *The Guns of Avalon*, *The Sign of the Unicorn*, *The Hand of Oberon*, and *The Courts of Chaos*. This complex series of novels weaves threads of political intrigue, the Tarot, magic, swordplay, and the nature of reality into a semi-Gordian knot that the careful reader can untie. Amber is the only true reality, and all other worlds, including our own, are but shadows of that one. When Oberon, the ruler of the kingdom of Amber, disappears, the crown is up for grabs between the nine princes of the realm. Prince Corwin is the protagonist, and the series follows his attempts to gain the throne, fight off his brothers' tries at succession, find out what or who or when happened to his father, and keep all the realities from collapsing into chaos. It's a complicated series, but worth the effort for the reader who likes a challenge.

Zelazny is as well respected for his short stories as for his novels, and one of his most popular characters is Colonel Dilvish of Dilvar, a man who has spent two centuries enduring the torments of Hell, and then returns to the land of the living. These stories (and the Dilvish novel *The Changing Land*) might be called "thinking persons' sword-and-sorcery," emphasizing character and mood rather than blood and guts. Stories of Zelazny's not in the Dilvish series include the humorous "The George Business" and the modern Arthurian fantasy "The Last Defender of Camelot."

Zelazny is one of the better writers in the science-fiction/fantasy field, and all of the above stories are infused with his particular poetic style, imagery flowing freely; the Dilvish stories are a slight departure, being almost impressionistic. For the reader who enjoys fine writing and a tinge of science fiction in fantasy, he is highly recommended. (b. 1937)

CHAPTER TWO

Ayesha To Zimiamvia— The Series of Fantasy

Any reader of fantasy cannot help but know that any given work in that field is, as likely as not, only a part of a whole. Sequels, trilogies, tetralogies, and series abound; what this causes in frustration at times is more than made up for by the knowledge that there is more to be read about a favorite character or place.

The series of fantasy, as in detective fiction, can be woven around a memorable character, such as Haggard's She, or group of characters—the Moomintroll family and their endless friends and relations. Or, as in science fiction, a place will be the continuing factor: a castle (Gormenghast), a country (Oz), a continent (Atlan), a world (Middle-Earth), a universe (Cthulhu's space-time), or just a neighborhood bar (Gavagan's).

Perhaps more questions are asked at The Science Fiction Shop about the components of series than any other matter (except the dreaded "What's good?" of course). In this section, we will try to give the parts of as many wholes as possible. We have defined a series as consisting of three books or more; in the case of books that have only one sequel, both are almost always mentioned by name in the pieces on the individual authors. In the case where it is a series of short stories that have gone to make up only one or two books, again they will be mentioned in the author section. And in a canon, where the linking matter is purely referential, as in Lovecraft's Cthulhu mythos, where there is no particular sequence or continuity, there seemed little point in making a list that would purely be a matter of the order in which the stories were published.

The frustration mentioned above is occasioned by the lack of availability of one or more of a series that the reader is well into. This is particularly horrendous when the series is an ongoing story, such as *The Lord of the Rings* or the "Riddle-Master of Hed" trilogy.

We wish we had a sure answer for this problem. Here, at least, you will be able to find out the titles you may be missing. Then a knowledgeable bookseller or librarian should be able to tell you if they are still in print. The conscientious publisher will try to keep all the titles of a series available, but the complexities of publishing sometime preclude this. In that case, one must burrow through every stack of secondhand books one comes across, or contact the (usually) reputable dealers in rare and out-of-print books who advertise in the science-fiction and fantasy periodicals.

Despite this drawback, though, its series are a major factor in the richness of fantasy. One of the more wondrous things in a wondrous field is that more often than not, of all the series you will find listed on the following pages, the second, third, fourth, ad infinitum, will be as good as the first.

JOAN AIKEN

The Alternate England Series
1. *The Wolves of Willoughby Chase*
2. *Black Hearts In Battersea*
3. *Nightbirds On Nantucket*
4. *The Stolen Lake*
5. *The Cuckoo Tree*
6. *The Whispering Mountain* (not directly related to series, but in same world)

LLOYD ALEXANDER

The Chronicles of Prydain Series
1. *The Book of Three*
2. *The Black Cauldron*
3. *The Castle of Llyr*
4. *Taran Wanderer*
5. *The High King*
6. *The Foundling*—short stories

PIERS ANTHONY

The Magic of Xanth Series
1. *A Spell for Chameleon*
2. *The Source of the Magic*
3. *Castle Roogna*
4. *Centaur Aisle*

The Proton/Phaze Trilogy
1. *Split Infinity*
2. *The Blue Adept*
3. *Juxtaposition*

ROBERT ASPRIN

The Mythic Persons Series
1. *Another Fine Myth*
2. *Myth Conceptions*
3. *Myth Direction* (tentative title)
4. *Hit or Myth* (tentative title)

L. FRANK BAUM

The Oz Books
1. *The Wizard of Oz*
2. *The Land of Oz*
3. *Ozma of Oz*
4. *Dorothy and the Wizard in Oz*

5. *The Road to Oz*
6. *The Emerald City of Oz*
7. *The Patchwork Girl of Oz*
8. *Til-Tok of Oz*
9. *The Scarecrow of Oz*
10. *Rinkitink in Oz*
11. *The Lost Princess of Oz*
12. *The Tin Woodman of Oz*
13. *The Magic of Oz*
14. *Glinda of Oz*

By Ruth Plumly Thompson:
15. *The Royal Book of Oz*
16. *Kabumpo in Oz*
17. *The Cowardly Lion of Oz*
18. *Grampa in Oz*
19. *The Lost King of Oz*
20. *The Hungry Tiger of Oz*
21. *The Gnome King of Oz*
22. *The Giant Horse of Oz*
23. *Jack Pumpkinhead of Oz*
24. *The Yellow Knight of Oz*
25. *Pirates in Oz*
26. *The Purple Prince of Oz*
27. *Ojo in Oz*
28. *Speedy in Oz*
29. *The Wishing Horse of Oz*
30. *Captain Salt in Oz*
31. *Handy Mandy in Oz*
32. *The Silver Princess in Oz*
33. *Ozoplaning with the Wizard of Oz*
(Also by Ruth Plumly Thompson: *Yankee in Oz*, published by the International Wizard of Oz Club)

By John R. Neill:
34. *The Wonder City of Oz*
35. *The Scalawagons of Oz*
36. *Lucky Bucky in Oz*

By Jack Snow:
37. *The Magical Mimics in Oz*

38. *The Shaggy Man of Oz*
(Also by Jack Snow: *Who's Who in Oz*)

By Rachel Cosgrove:
39. *The Hidden Valley of Oz*

By Eloise Jarvas McGraw and Lauren McGraw Wagner:
40. *Merry Go Round in Oz*

JOHN BELLAIRS

The Lewis Barnavelt Series
1. *The House with a Clock in Its Walls*
2. *The Figure in the Shadows*
3. *The Letter, the Witch, and the Ring*

JAMES BLISH

After Such Knowledge
1. *Doctor Mirabilis*
2. *Black Easter*
3. *The Day after Judgment*
4. *A Case of Conscience*

JAMES BRANCH CABELL

The Biography of Manuel of Poictesme Series
1. *Beyond Life: Dizaine des Demiurges*
2. *Figures of Earth: A Comedy of Appearances*
3. *The Silver Stallion: A Comedy of Redemption*
4. *The Witch Woman: A Trilogy about Her*
5. *The Soul of Melicent*
6. *Chivalry*
7. *Jurgen: A Comedy of Justice*
8. *The Line of Love*
9. *The High Place: A Comedy of Disenchantment*
10. *Gallantry: An Eighteenth-Century Dizain in Ten Comedies with an Afterpiece*

11. *Something about Eve: A Comedy of Fig-Leaves*
12. *The Certain Hour (Dizaine des Poetes)*
13. *The Cords of Vanity: A Comedy of Shirking*
14. *From the Hidden Way: Being Seventy-five Adaptations*
15. *The Jewel Merchants: A Comedy in One Act*
16. *The Rivet in Grandfather's Neck: A Comedy of Limitations*
17. *The Eagle's Shadow*
18. *The Cream of the Jest: A Comedy of Evasions*
19. *The Lineage of Lichfield: An Essay in Eugenics*
20. *Straws and Prayer Books: Dizain des Diversions*

MOYRA CALDECOTT

The Tall Stones Series
1. *The Tall Stones*
2. *The Temple of the Sun*
3. *Shadow on the Stones*

LIN CARTER

The Green Star Series
1. *Under the Green Star*
2. *When the Green Star Calls*
3. *By the Light of the Green Star*
4. *As the Green Star Rises*
5. *In the Green Star's Glow*

The Thongor Series
1. *The Wizard of Lemuria* (revised and expanded as *Thongor and the Wizard of Lemuria*)
2. *Thongor of Lemuria* (revised and expanded as *Thongor and the Dragon City*)
3. *Thongor against the Gods*
4. *Thongor in the City of Magicians*
5. *Thongor at the End of Time*
6. *Thongor Fights the Pirates of Tarakus*

The World's End Series
1. *The Warrior of World's End*
2. *The Enchantress of World's End*
3. *The Immortal of World's End*
4. *The Barbarian of World's End*
5. *The Pirate of World's End*

The Zarkon Trilogy
1. *Invisible Death*
2. *The Nemesis of Evil*
3. *The Volcano Ogre*

VERA CHAPMAN

The Three Damosels Trilogy
1. *The Green Knight*
2. *The King's Damosel*
3. *King Arthur's Daughter*

SUSAN COOPER

The Dark Is Rising Sequence
1. *Over Sea, Under Stone*
2. *The Dark Is Rising*
3. *Greenwitch*
4. *Grey King*
5. *Silver on the Tree*

L. SPRAGUE DE CAMP and FLETCHER PRATT

The Harold Shea Stories
1. *The Incomplete Enchanter*
2. *The Castle of Iron*
3. *The Wall of Serpents*

(NOTE: The Shea series needs a bit of explanation, since the books have been divided and titled in several ways. *The*

Incomplete Enchanter is made up of two novelettes, "The Roaring Trumpet" and "The Mathematics of Magic." It and *The Castle of Iron* have appeared in one volume as *The Compleat Enchanter. The Wall of Serpents* also consists of two novelettes, "The Wall of Serpents" and "The Green Magician" and has also appeared as *The Enchanter Compleated.*)

GRAHAM DIAMOND

The Haven Series
1. *The Haven*
2. *Lady of the Haven*
3. *Dungeons of Kuba*
4. *The Falcons of Eden*
5. *The Beasts of Hades*

(NOTE: Novels 2, 3, 4, and 5 are also known as the Adventures of the Empire Princess Series.)

PETER DICKINSON

The Changes Trilogy
1. *The Devil's Children*
2. *Heartsease*
3. *The Weathermonger*

STEPHEN R. DONALDSON

The Chronicles of Thomas Covenant
First Chronicles
1. *Lord Foul's Bane*

2. *The Illearth War*[1]
3. *The Power That Preserves*

Second Chronicles
1. *The Wounded Land*
2. *The One Tree*
3. *The White Gold Wielder*

Third Chronicles
These three are not as yet titled.

LORD DUNSANY

The Jorkens Stories
1. *Jorkens Remembers Africa*
2. *Jorkens Has a Large Whiskey*
3. *Jorkens Borrows Another Whiskey*
4. *The Fourth Book of Jorkens*

EDWARD EAGER

The Half Magic Series
1. *Half Magic*
2. *Knight's Castle*
3. *Magic by the Lake*
4. *The Time Garden*

E. R. EDDISON

The Zimiamvian Trilogy
1. *The Mezentian Gate*
2. *A Fish Dinner in Memison*
3. *Mistress of Mistresses*

(The opinion is generally held that this trilogy should be

---

[1]*Gilden-Fire*, published by a small press, is a chapter of this novel that did not originally appear in print.

read in the above order, which follows the interior chronology, even though it was published in exactly opposite sequence.)

GARDNER F. FOX

Kothar
1. *Kothar—Barbarian Swordsman*
2. *Kothar of the Magic Sword!*
3. *Kothar and the Demon Queen*
4. *Kothar and the Conjurer's Curse*
5. *Kothar and the Wizard Slayer*

Kyrik
1. *Kyrik: Warlock Warrior*
2. *Kyrik Fights the Demon World*
3. *Kyrik and the Wizard's Sword*
4. *Kyrik and the Lost Queen*

JANE GASKELL

The Atlan Saga
1. *The Serpent*
2. *The Dragon*
3. *Atlan*
4. *The City*
5. *Some Summer Lands*

(NOTE: Originally *The Serpent* and *The Dragon* appeared in the U.S. and England as one volume, *The Serpent*. Gaskell's earlier work, *King's Daughter*, takes place in the same world as that of the Atlan Saga, but there is otherwise no connection.)

ROLAND GREEN

The Wandor Series
1. *Wandor's Ride*

2. *Wandor's Journey*
3. *Wandor's Voyage*
4. *Wandor's Flight*
5. *Wandor's Battle*

H. RIDER HAGGARD

The She Novels
1. *Wisdom's Daughter*
2. *She and Allan*
3. *She*
4. *Ayesha, the Return of She*

(NOTE: There are about 15 novels devoted to Allan Quatermain, some of which are fantasies, some of which are pure adventure.)

NEIL HANCOCK

The Circle of Light Series
1. *Circle of Light 1: Greyfax Grimwald*
2. *Circle of Light 2: Faragon Fairingay*
3. *Circle of Light 3: Calix Stay*
4. *Circle of Light 4: Squaring the Circle*

PAUL HAZEL

The Finnbranch
1. *Yearwood*
2. *Undersea*
3. *Winterking*

ROBERT E. HOWARD

The Conan Series
(As noted in the text, Howard's works are the despair of bibliographers and readers alike. The following seems to

173

be a generally accepted order of the "original" Conan books, most of which consist of several short stories. Authorship is usually credited to Howard and L. Sprague de Camp and/or Lin Carter. There were hard-cover Conans published in the 1950s which were different permutations of the stories, collectors' editions devoted to only the Howard material, and at least one entirely separate Conan series with no material by Howard at all.)

1. *Conan*
2. *Conan of Cimmeria*
3. *Conan the Freebooter*
4. *Conan the Wanderer*
5. *Conan the Adventurer*
6. *Conan the Buccaneer*
7. *Conan the Warrior*
8. *Conan the Usurper*
9. *Conan the Conquerer*
10. *Conan the Avenger*
11. *Conan of Aquilonia*
12. *Conan of the Isles*

The Solomon Kane Tales

1. *The Moon of Skulls*
2. *The Hand of Kane*
3. *Solomon Kane*

JOHN JAKES

Brak the Barbarian Series

1. *Brak the Barbarian*
2. *Brak the Barbarian Versus the Sorceress*
3. *Brak the Barbarian Versus the Mark of the Demon*
4. *The Fortunes of Brak*

TOVE JANSSON

The Moomin Books

1. *Finn Family Moomintroll*
2. *Comet in Moominland*

3. *The Exploits of Moominpappa*
4. *Moominsummer Madness*
5. *Moominland Midwinter*
6. *Tales from Moomin Valley*
7. *Moominpappa at Sea*

DIANA WYNNE JONES

The Dalemark Sequence
1. *Drowned Ammet*
2. *Cart and Cwidder*
3. *The Spellcoats*

RICHARD KIRK

Raven Series
1. *Raven 1: Swordsmistress of Chaos*
2. *Raven 2: A Time of Ghosts*
3. *Raven 3: The Frozen God*
4. *Raven 4: Lords of the Shadows*
5. *Raven 5: A Time of Dying*

KATHERINE KURTZ

The Chronicles of the Deryni
1. *Deryni Rising*
2. *Deryni Checkmate*
3. *High Deryni*

The Legends of Camber of Culdi
1. *Camber of Culdi*
2. *Saint Camber*
3. *Camber the Heretic*

R. A. LAFFERTY

The Devil Is Dead Trilogy
1. *Archipelago*
2. *The Devil Is Dead*
3. *More Than Melchisedech* (projected)

TANITH LEE

The Demon Lord Series
1. *Night's Master*
2. *Death's Master*
3. *Delusion's Master*

The Birthgrave Series
1. *The Birthgrave*
2. *Vazkor, Son of Vazkor*
3. *Quest for the White Witch*

URSULA K. LE GUIN

The Earthsea Trilogy
1. *A Wizard of Earthsea*
2. *The Tombs of Atuan*
3. *The Farthest Shore*

FRITZ LEIBER

The Fafhrd and the Gray Mouser Series
1. *Swords and Deviltry*
2. *Swords against Death*
3. *Swords in the Mist*
4. *Swords against Wizardry*
5. *The Swords of Lankhmar*
6. *Swords and Ice Magic*

(NOTE: This series is made up of many short stories and a novel which is an expansion of a shorter magazine version

[*The Swords of Lankhmar*]. There are several other Fafhrd and Gray Mouser books, which consist essentially of material available in the basic six listed above.)

C. S. LEWIS

The Chronicles of Narnia
1. *The Lion, the Witch, and the Wardrobe*
2. *Prince Caspian*
3. *The Voyage of the Dawn Treader*
4. *The Silver Chair*
5. *The Horse and His Boy*
6. *The Magician's Nephew*
7. *The Last Battle*

HUGH LOFTING

The Doctor Doolittle Series
1. *The Story of Doctor Doolittle*
2. *The Voyages of Doctor Doolittle (Doctor Doolittle and the Pirates)*
3. *Doctor Doolittle's Post Office*
4. *Doctor Doolittle's Circus*
5. *Doctor Doolittle's Zoo*
6. *Doctor Doolittle's Caravan*
7. *Doctor Doolittle's Garden*
8. *Doctor Doolittle in the Moon*
9. *Doctor Doolittle's Return*
10. *Doctor Doolittle and the Secret Lake*
11. *Doctor Doolittle and the Green Canary*
12. *Doctor Doolittle's Puddleby Adventure*

BRIAN LUMLEY

The Titus Crow Series
1. *The Burrowers Beneath*
2. *The Transition of Titus Crow*
3. *The Clock of Dreams*

4. *Spawn of the Winds*
5. *In the Moons of Borea*

GEORGE MacDONALD

The Curdie Series
1. *At the Back of the North Wind*
2. *The Princess and the Goblin*
3. *The Princess and Curdie*

PATRICIA McKILLIP

The Riddle-Master Trilogy
1. *The Riddle-Master of Hed*
2. *Heir of Sea and Fire*
3. *Harpist in the Wind*

MICHAEL MOORCOCK

The Elric Series
1. *Elric of Melnibone (The Dreaming City)*
2. *A Sailor on the Seas of Fate*
3. *The Weird of the White Wolf (The Stealer of Souls)*
4. *The Vanishing Tower (The Sleeping Sorceress)*
5. *The Bane of the Black Sword*
6. *Stormbringer*

The Runestaff Series
1. *The Jewel in the Skull*
2. *The Mad God's Amulet*
3. *The Sword of the Dawn*
4. *The Runestaff*

Castle Brass Series
1. *Count Brass*
2. *Champion of Garathorn*
3. *The Quest for Tanelorn*

Chronicles of Corum
1. *The Knight of Swords*
2. *The Queen of Swords*
3. *The King of Swords*
4. *The Bull and the Spear*
5. *The Oak and the Ram*
6. *The Sword and the Stallion*

(NOTE: The first three are collected under the title *The Swords Trilogy*, and the last three as *The Chronicles of Corum*.)

John Daker Series
1. *The Eternal Champion*
2. *The Silver Warriors*

TALBOT MUNDY

The Jimgrim Series
1. *Jimgrim and Allah's Peace*
2. *The Seventeen Rifles of El-Kalil*
3. *The Lion of Petra*
4. *The Woman Ayisha*
5. *The Lost Trooper*
6. *The King in Check*
7. *The Mystery of Khufu's Tomb*
8. *The Hundred Days*
9. *The Nine Unknown*
10. *The Devil's Guard*
11. *Jimgrim*

H. WARNER MUNN

The Merlin Family Saga
1. *King of the World's Edge*
2. *The Ship from Atlantis*
3. *Merlin's Godson*

(NOTE: The first two are combined in the volume *Merlin's Ring*.)

179

Tales of the Werewolf Clan
1. *The Werewolf of Ponkert*
2. *Tales of the Werewolf Clan 1*
3. *Tales of the Werewolf Clan 2*

EDITH NESBIT

The Five Children
1. *The Five Children and It*
2. *The Phoenix and the Carpet*
3. *The Story of the Amulet*

ANDRE NORTON

The Witch World Series
1. *Witch World*
2. *Web of the Witch World*
3. *Year of the Unicorn*
4. *Three against the Witch World*
5. *Warlock of the Witch World*
6. *Sorceress of the Witch World*
7. *Spell of the Witch World* (short-story collection)
8. *The Crystal Gryphon*
9. *Gryphon in Glory*
10. *The Jargoon Pard*
11. *The Trey of Swords* (short-story collection)
12. *Zarsthor's Bane*
13. *Lore of the Witch World* (short-story collection)

ANDREW OFFUTT

Tiana's Trilogy
1. *The Demon in the Mirror*
2. *The Eyes of Sarsis*
3. *The Web of the Spider*

The Cormac Mac Art Series
1. *The Sword of the Gael*

2. *The Undying Wizard*
3. *The Sign of the Moonbow*
4. *The Mists of Doom*

MERVYN PEAKE

The Gormenghast Trilogy
1. *Titus Groan*
2. *Gormenghast*
3. *Titus Alone*

SEABURY QUINN

The Jules deGrandin Series
1. *The Phantom Fighter*
2. *The Adventures of Jules deGrandin*
3. *The Casebook of Jules deGrandin*
4. *The Skeleton Closet of Jules deGrandin*
5. *The Devil's Bride*
6. *The Hellfire Files of Jules deGrandin*
7. *The Horror Chamber of Jules deGrandin*

(Six of the above are short-story collections, while *The Devil's Bride* is a novel.)

FRED SABERHAGEN

The Dracula Series
1. *The Dracula Tapes*
2. *The Holmes-Dracula File*
3. *An Old Friend of the Family*
4. *Thorn*

NANCY SPRINGER

The Chronicles of Isle
1. *The White Hart*

2. *The Silver Sun*
3. *The Sable Moon*

ROBERT STALLMAN

The Book of the Beast
1. *The Orphan*
2. *The Captive*
3. *The Book of the Beast*

MARY STEWART

The Life of Merlin
1. *The Crystal Cave*
2. *The Hollow Hills*
3. *The Last Enchantment*

RUTH PLUMLY THOMPSON
(See listing of Oz books under L. FRANK BAUM)

J. R. R. TOLKIEN

The Chronicles of Middle-Earth
1. *The Silmarillion*
2. *Unfinished Tales*
3. *The Hobbit*
4. *The Lord of the Rings*
     1. *The Fellowship of the Ring*
     2. *The Two Towers*
     3. *The Return of the King*

P. L. TRAVERS

The Mary Poppins Books
1. *Mary Poppins*
2. *Mary Poppins Comes Back*

3. *Mary Poppins Opens the Door*
4. *Mary Poppins in the Park*

KARL EDWARD WAGNER

The Kane Series
1. *Darkness Weaves with Many Shades*
2. *Death Angel's Shadow*
3. *Bloodstone*
4. *Dark Crusade*
5. *Night Winds*

HUGH WALKER

The Magira Series
1. *War Gamers' World*
2. *Army of Darkness*
3. *Messengers of Darkness*

EVANGELINE WALTON

The Mabinogi Series
1. *The Prince of Annwm*
2. *The Children of Llyr*
3. *The Song of Rhiannon*
4. *The Island of the Mighty*

MANLY WADE WELLMAN

The Silver John Series
1. *Who Fears the Devil?*
2. *The Old Gods Waken*
3. *After Dark*
4. *The Lost and the Lurking*

T. H. WHITE

The Arthur Stories (original versions)
1. *The Sword in the Stone*
2. *The Witch in the Wood*
3. *The Ill-Made Knight*

(Revised and expanded into *The Once and Future King*)

4. *The Book of Merlyn*

LEONARD WIBBERLY

The Mouse Series
1. *Beware of the Mouse*
2. *The Mouse That Roared*
3. *The Mouse on the Moon*
4. *The Mouse on Wall Street*

CHELSEA QUINN YARBRO

The Count de Saint-Germain Series
1. *Hotel Transylvania*
2. *The Palace*
3. *Blood Games*
4. *Path of the Eclipse*
5. *Tempting Fate*

ROGER ZELAZNY

The Amber Quintet
1. *Nine Princes in Amber*
2. *The Guns of Avalon*
3. *The Sign of the Unicorn*
4. *The Hand of Oberon*
5. *The Courts of Chaos*

CHAPTER THREE

Beyond the Fields
We Know,
There and Back Again,
That Old Black Magic

In case you don't know, the three phrases in the title of this section refer, respectively, to the beautifully felicitous phrase of Lord Dunsany's, the subtitle of *The Hobbit*, and the title of a well-known popular song.

We have chosen these, with three others, to characterize various divisions into which most fantasy seems naturally to fall. In our *A Reader's Guide to Science Fiction*, we used individual guidelines with most of the author pieces to suggest that if you like A's work, you might well check out B. But fantasy doesn't seem to lend itself to that sort of linkage. At The Science Fiction Shop, where most science-fiction queries are for writers similar to other writers, the questions *re* fantasy are more for type.

So we have divided most of the works mentioned in the other parts of this book into six categories (some are absolutely unclassifiable). They are as follows:

1. There and Back Again. As noted, that is the subtitle of *The Hobbit*, which doesn't fall into this section. Nevertheless, it is a perfect description of this particular sort of story, in which someone from our world ventures, falls, or is abducted into another, more magical world. Exemplary works are *The Wizard of Oz*, *The Ship of Ishtar* (Merritt), and *Red Moon and Black Mountain* (Chant).

2. Beyond the Fields We Know. That lovely phrase of Lord Dunsany's describes those works which take place entirely in magic worlds, with no concrete links to our own time and place. Well-known works of this sort are *The Lord of the Rings* (Tolkien) and the "Elric" series (Moorcock).

3. Unicorns in the Garden. We have paraphrased the title of Thurber's famous story to characterize those tales in which magical and fantastic events occur in our mundane world. Examples range from the cockeyed ghosts of *Topper* (Smith) to that strangest of tent shows, *The Circus of Dr. Lao* (C. G. Finney).

4. That Old Black Magic. This category is really a subdivision of the preceding one, but stories in which the everyday is menaced by the supernatural to inspire fright and horror are a class by themselves; alas, the unknown is still terrifying to most of humanity, thus that most venerable of all fantasies, the ghost story, from *Dracula* (Stoker) to *The Shining* (King).

5. Bambi's Children. The most famous of stories in which animals think, speak, and act with human intelligence is *Bambi* (Salten). There was indeed a sequel entitled *Bambi's Children,* but there are other works that also belong in this small but distinct category.

6. Once and Future Kings, Queens, and Heroes. Finally, there are the stories that have been handed down from time immemorial, the great legends of many cultures, which have been used by contemporary authors to provide new insights into the ancient myths or into our own time. The tales of Arthur and Camelot have perhaps been mined the most, and the most famous example of these must be *The Once and Future King.*

Further subdivisions are possible; we debated the fact that category number 2, Beyond the Fields We Know, could be further divided into what might be thought of as "barbarian" (i.e. Conan and his clones) and "civilized" (Hed) exotic locales, but once started into subdivision, there was a suspicion we might never be able to stop. So here are our six major kinds of fantasy; if one or more are a favorite of yours, we hope that this might lead you to further adventures in that area.

1. There and Back Again

Almuric	Robert E. Howard
A Midsummer Tempest	Poul Anderson
The Amber Quintet	Roger Zelazny
At the Back of the North Wind	George MacDonald
The Chronicles of Thomas Covenant the Unbeliever	Stephen R. Donaldson
The Chronicles of Narnia	C. S. Lewis
The Cloud Forest	Joan North
The Dark World	Henry Kuttner
The Dragon and the George	Gordon R. Dickson
The Dream Quest of Unknown Kadath	H. P. Lovecraft
Glory Road	Robert A. Heinlein
The Green Star Series	Lin Carter
The Half Magic Series	Edward Eager
The Harold Shea Stories	L. Sprague de Camp and Fletcher Pratt
The Haunted Woman	David Lindsay
Inferno	Larry Niven and Jerry Pournelle
The King of Elfland's Daughter	Lord Dunsany
The Land of Unreason	L. Sprague de Camp and Fletcher Pratt
The Light Maze	Joan North
Lilith	George MacDonald
The Little White Bird	J. M. Barrie
The Mythic Persons Series	Robert Asprin
Operation Chaos	Poul Anderson
The Oz Books	L. Brank Baum
Peter Pan	J. M. Barrie
Peter Pan in Kensington Gardens	J. M. Barrie
Phantastes	George MacDonald
Red Moon and Black Mountain	Joy Chant
Seven Day Magic	Edward Eager
The Ship of Ishtar	A. Merritt

Smith of Wootton Major	J. R. R. Tolkien
The Sorcerer's Ship	Hannes Bok
Steel Magic	Andre Norton
Strange Evil	Jane Gaskell
Three Hearts and Three Lions	Poul Anderson
The Whirling Shapes	Joan North
The Woodrow Wilson Dime	Jack Finney
The Zimiamvian Trilogy	E. R. Eddison

2. Beyond the Fields We Know

Alternate England Series	Joan Aiken
The Alyx Stories	Joanna Russ
The Atlan Saga	Jane Gaskell
The Biography of Manuel of Poictesme Series	James Branch Cabell
The Black God's Shadow	C. L. Moore
The Blue Hawk	Peter Dickinson
The Blue Star	Fletcher Pratt
Born to Exile	Phyllis Eisenstein
Brak the Barbarian Series	John Jakes
The Broken Sword	Poul Anderson
The Cat Who Wanted To Be A Man	Lloyd Alexander
The Changing Land	Roger Zelazny
Charmed Life	Diana Wynne Jones
The Chronicles of Corum	Michael Moorcock
Chronicles of the Deryni	Katherine Kurtz
The Chronicles of Isle	Nancy Springer
The Chronicles of Middle-Earth	J. R. R. Tolkien
The Chronicles of Prydain	Lloyd Alexander
The Clocks of Iraz	L. Sprague de Camp
Come, Lady Death	Peter S. Beagle
The Conan Series	Robert E. Howard and others
The Dalemark Sequence	Diana Wynne Jones
The Dark World	Henry Kuttner

3. Unicorns in the Garden

A Fine and Private Place	Peter S. Beagle
Alien Flesh	Seabury Quinn
All Hallows' Eve	Charles Williams
Beauty	Robin McKinley
Black Easter/The Day after Judgment	James Blish
Blind Voices	Tom Reamy
The Boats of the Glen Carrig	William Hope Hodgson
The Book of the Beast	Robert Stallman
The Box of Delights	John Masefield
The Charwoman's Shadow	Lord Dunsany
The Circus of Dr. Lao	Charles G. Finney
Cormac Mac Art Series	Andrew Offutt
The Crock of Gold	James Stephens
Dark Horn Blowing	Dahlov Ipcar
The Dark Is Rising Sequence	Susan Cooper
Descent into Hell	Charles Williams
The Devil on the Road	Robert Westall
The Devil Wives of Li Fong	E. Hoffman Price
Devil's Children	Peter Dickinson
Dogsbody	Diana Wynne Jones
Don Rodriguez	Lord Dunsany
Dragon Magic	Andre Norton
The Drawing of the Dark	Tim Powers
Earthfasts	William Mayne
Eight Days of Luke	Diana Wynne Jones
The Elephant and the Kangaroo	T. H. White
Elidor	Alan Garner
The Enchanted Castle	E. Nesbit
Excalibur	Sanders Anne Laubenthal
The Face That Must Die	Ramsey Campbell
The Five Children Trilogy	E. Nesbit
The Flight of the Horse	Larry Niven
For the Witch of the Mists	David C. Smith
Fur Magic	Andre Norton
The Glorious Pool	Thorne Smith

The Greater Trumps	Charles Williams
Harding's Luck	E. Nesbit
Harkfast	Hugh C. Rae
Hasan	Piers Anthony
Heartsease	Peter Dickinson
The Hill Road	William Mayne
Hobberdy Dick	K. M. Briggs
The House of Arden	E. Nesbit
If You Could See Me Now	Peter Straub
It	William Mayne
The Jimgrim Series	Talbot Mundy
The Jorkens Stories	Lord Dunsany
Kate Crackernuts	K. M. Briggs
The Lastborn of Elvinwood	Linda Haldeman
Lavender-Green Magic	Andre Norton
Lazy Bear Lane	Thorne Smith
The Lewis Barnavelt Series	John Bellairs
Lila the Werewolf	Peter S. Beagle
Linnets and Valerians	Elizabeth Goudge
Little, Big	John Crowley
The Little White Horse	Elizabeth Goudge
The Magic Garden	E. Nesbit
The Magic Goes Away	Larry Niven
The Magician out of Manchuria	Charles G. Finney
Many Dimensions	Charles Williams
Many Moons	James Thurber
Marion's Wall	Jack Finney
The Mary Poppins Books	P. L. Travers
The Merlin Family Saga	H. Warner Munn
The Merman's Children	Poul Anderson
The Midnight Folk	John Masefield
Mistress Masham's Repose	T. H. White
The Moon of Gomrath	Alan Garner
Mr. Pye	Mervyn Peake
The Night Life of the Gods	Thorne Smith
Octagon Magic	Andre Norton
The Ogre Downstairs	Diana Wynne Jones
The Owl Service	Alan Garner
The Picture of Dorian Gray	Oscar Wilde
The Place of the Lion	Charles Williams

Portrait of Jennie	Robert Nathan
The Power of Three	Diana Wynne Jones
Puck of Pook's Hill	Rudyard Kipling
Rewards and Fairies	Rudyard Kipling
Samarkand	Graham Diamond
The Sea Lady	H. G. Wells
Shadow Land	Peter Straub
Shadows of Ecstasy	Charles Williams
The She Novels	H. Rider Haggard
The Silver John Series	Manly Wade Wellman
Skin and Bones	Thorne Smith
The Solomon Kane Tales	Robert E. Howard
Star of the Sea	Linda Haldeman
The Stray Lamb	Thorne Smith
Tales From Gavagan's Bar	L. Sprague de Camp and Fletcher Pratt
The Thief of Kalimir	Graham Diamond
The Thirteen Clocks	James Thurber
To Wake The Dead (U.S. Title: *The Parasite*)	Ramsey Campbell
Topper	Thorne Smith
The Treasure of the Isle of Mist	W. W. Tarn
Turnabout	Thorne Smith
The Unholy City	Charles G. Finney
The Violet Apple	David Lindsay
War in Heaven	Charles Williams
The Watch House	Robert Westall
The Weathermonger	Peter Dickinson
The Weirdstone of Brisingamen	Alan Garner
Wet Magic	E. Nesbit
The White Deer	James Thurber
The Wind Eye	Robert Westall
The Witch of the Indies	David C. Smith
Witch's Business (a.k.a. *Wilkin's Tooth*)	Diana Wynne Jones
The Wonderful O	James Thurber
The Wonderful Visit	H. G. Wells
The Zarkon Trilogy	Lin Carter

4. That Old Black Magic

Best Ghost Stories	Algernon Blackwood
Burn, Witch, Burn!	A. Merritt
The Burning Court	John Dickson Carr
Carrie	Stephen King
The Case of Charles Dexter Ward	H. P. Lovecraft
Conjure Wife	Fritz Leiber
Creep, Shadow!	A. Merritt
Dark Carnival	Ray Bradbury
The Doll Who Ate His Mother	Ramsey Campbell
Dracula	Bram Stoker
Dracula's Guest	Bram Stoker
The Ghost Pirates	William Hope Hodgson
Ghost Stories of an Antiquary	M. R. James
Ghost Story	Peter Straub
The Great White Space	Basil Copper
The House on the Borderland	William Hope Hodgson
The Jules deGrandin Series	Seabury Quinn
Kill the Dead	Tanith Lee
The King in Yellow	Robert W. Chambers
Lair of the White Worm	Bram Stoker
The Maker of Moons	Robert W. Chambers
Moonchild	Aleister Crowley
The October Country	Ray Bradbury
Salem's Lot	Stephen King
Seven Footprints to Satan	A. Merritt
The Shadow Over Innsmouth	H. P. Lovecraft
The Shining	Stephen King
The Slayer of Souls	Robert W. Chambers
Something Wicked This Way Comes	Ray Bradbury
The Stand	Stephen King
Strange Eons	Robert Bloch
Tales of the Werewolf Clan	H. Warner Munn
The Three Imposters	Arthur Machen

To Wake the Dead (a.k.a. *The Parasite*)	Ramsey Campbell

5. Bambi's Children

Adventures of the Empire Princess Series	Graham Diamond
Bambi	Felix Salten
Bambi's Children	Felix Salten
Ben and Me	Robert Lawson
The Circle of Light Series	Neil Hancock
The City Jungle	Felix Salten
Doctor Doolittle Series	Hugh Lofting
Dragon Winter	Neil Hancock
Fifteen Rabbits	Felix Salten
The Haven	Graham Diamond
Journey of Tapiola	Robert Nathan
The Jungle Books	Rudyard Kipling
Mr. Revere and I	Robert Lawson
The Plague Dogs	Richard Adams
Perri	Felix Salten
Rabbit Hill	Robert Lawson
The Reluctant Dragon	Kenneth Grahame
Watership Down	Richard Adams
The Wind in the Willows	Kenneth Grahame

6. Once And Future Kings, Queens, and Heros

Blaedud the Birdman	Vera Chapman
The Book of Merlyn	T. H. White
Captain Sinbad	Graham Diamond
Day of the Minotaur	Thomas Burnett Swann
The Fair	Robert Nathan
The Golden Gryphon Feather	Richard Purtill
Green Phoenix	Thomas Burnett Swann
How Are the Mighty Fallen	Thomas Burnett Swann
Huon of the Horn	Andre Norton
Lady of the Bees	Thomas Burnett Swann

The Life of Merlin Series	Mary Stewart
The Mabinogi Series	Evangeline Walton
Moondust	Thomas Burnett Swann
The Once and Future King	T. H. White
The Queen of Swords	Dahlov Ipcar
Roads	Seabury Quinn
Silver, Jewels and Jade	Elizabeth Norman
The Stolen Goddess	Richard Purtill
The Three Damosels Trilogy	Vera Chapman
Till We Have Faces	C. S. Lewis
To the Chapel Perilous	Naomi Mitchison

CHAPTER FOUR:
The Seven-League Shelf

We consider the following list of books to be the cream of the crop, a basic reading-and-acquisition list for the lover of fantasy. It is meant to represent not only quality but breadth of taste and, to a degree, historical depth. You'll find every kind of fantasy represented and many of those works that have remained popular enough over the years to qualify as classics.

Any such list is subjective and there will be moans from the sidelines because certain treasured titles have not been included. But the three authors of this volume do have relatively divergent tastes, and the works selected are those we know to be important to the field and/or those we consistently recommend at The Science Fiction Shop. The method of selection began with each of us drawing up a list of his or her own nominations. Those titles that received multiple nominations were automatically included; those that received only one nomination were considered one by one and included only when all had agreed to its status. (This process was not without acrimony, but we are all speaking to each other again.)

A few observations on the list:

It will be noted that several of the selections are multiple volumes. "The Riddle-Master Trilogy," for instance, is a continuing story and essentially one long novel. On the other hand, there was no way in the world to make a judgmental selection of Tolkien's stories of Middle-Earth, so they're all included under the arbitrary title of "The Chronicles of Middle-Earth," by which we mean *The Hobbit, The Lord of the Rings, The Silmarillion,* and *Unfinished Tales.*

Bradbury was a problem, because it was felt that he deserved representation on the list, but no particular collection or novel was thought to be that typical. *Dark Carnival*, his first book, was chosen because of its historical importance, but it should be noted that that volume is now a collectors' item, bringing a large price on the rare-book market. Most of the stories in it can be found in *The October Country*, however.

Lovecraft put us in something of the same dilemma, but we decided that *The Shadow over Innsmouth* was long enough to qualify as a major work and satisfyingly representative of his best writings.

We have selected both Alan Garner's *The Weirdstone of Brisingamen* and its sequel, *The Moon of Gomrath*, though they are not strictly a continuous narrative, because we felt that the first book was just a shade too typically a juvenile, a quality which the second transcended. Nonetheless, it would have been silly to recommend only the sequel.

There are literally thousands of anthologies devoted to stories of the supernatural, but *Great Tales of Terror and the Supernatural*, of all of them, has stood the test of time as a brilliant sampler of the best. Curiously enough, there are almost no anthologies devoted to pure fantasy, and certainly none so definitive.

All of us felt that the original versions of the three novels that make up most of T. H. White's *The Once and Future King* were superior to the rewrites that went into the omnibus volume, but we listed the later version for simplicity's sake. For more on this, see the article on White.

Finally, while we certainly hope that this list will lead the novice reader of fantasy to many pleasures, might we suggest that even the experienced reader might benefit by casting an eye over it and taking a little test as to how many have been read. You might find that you've been limiting yourself.

The Seven-League Shelf

Poul Anderson, *The Broken Sword*
L. Frank Baum, *The Wizard of Oz*
Peter S. Beagle, *The Last Unicorn*
Ray Bradbury, *Dark Carnival*
Lewis Carroll, *Alice's Adventures in Wonderland*
Lord Dunsany, *The King of Elfland's Daughter*
Charles G. Finney, *The Circus of Dr. Lao*
Alan Garner, *The Wierdstone of Brisingamen;*
    The Moon of Gomrath
Jane Gaskell, The Atlan Saga
Kenneth Grahame, *The Wind in the Willows*
H. Rider Haggard, *She*
William Hope Hodgson, *The House on the Borderland*
Robert E. Howard, *Conan*
M. R. James, *Ghost Stories of an Antiquary*
Rudyard Kipling, The Jungle Books
Fritz Leiber, The Fafhrd and the Gray Mouser Series
C. S. Lewis, *Till We Have Faces*
H. P. Lovecraft, *The Shadow over Innsmouth*
George MacDonald, *Gifts of the Christ Child*
Patricia McKillip, The Riddle-Master Trilogy
A. Merritt, *The Ship of Ishtar*
Naomi Mitchison, *To the Chapel Perilous*
Michael Moorcock, The Elric Series
C. L. Moore, *The Black God's Shadow* (the Jirel of Joiry
    stories)
Edith Nesbit, *The Five Children and It*
Mervyn Peake, The Gormenghast Trilogy
Edgar Allan Poe, *The Fall of the House of Usher*
Bram Stoker, *Dracula*
J. R. R. Tolkien, The Chronicles of Middle-Earth
T. H. White, *The Once and Future King*
Charles Williams, *War in Heaven*
Herbert A. Wise and Phyllis Fraser, Eds., *Great Tales of*
    Terror and the Supernatural
Austin Tappan Wright, *Islandia*

CHAPTER FIVE:
Half My Daughter and the Hand of My Kingdom

OK. OK. OK. We know it's really the other way around, but we wanted to indicate that literary awards are only partially as reliable as that oldest of prizes inevitably won by killing the dragon. In this section, you will find a listing of the recipients of the major awards in fantasy. Because fantasy as a viable genre is so recent, the lists are sparse. And remember that, while a prizewinner obviously has something to offer or it wouldn't have won, all the awards in fantasy are voted by the membership of various conventions, therefore making them on one hand the selection of a relatively few people, and on the other a popular poll, as opposed, for instance, to science fiction's Nebula Award, which is decided by the Science Fiction Writers of America, the author's peers.

GANDALF AWARD
Awarded by the World Science Fiction Convention, in conjunction with the Hugo Awards. This award is in recognition of contributions to Fantasy, and is a "Grand Master" award.

1974: J. R. R. Tolkien
1975: Fritz Leiber
1976: L. Sprague de Camp
1977: Andre Norton
1978: Poul Anderson
1979: Ursula K. Le Guin
1980: Ray Bradbury

WORLD FANTASY AWARDS
Awarded yearly by the World Fantasy Convention.

First World Fantasy Awards (1975)
BEST NOVEL: *The Forgotten Beasts of Eld*, by Patricia McKillip
BEST SHORT FICTION: "Pages from a Young Girl's Diary," by Robert Aickman
BEST ANTHOLOGY/COLLECTION: *Worse Things Waiting*, by Manly Wade Wellman
LIFE ACHIEVEMENT AWARD: Robert Bloch

Second World Fantasy Awards (1976)
BEST NOVEL: *Bid Time Return*, by Richard Matheson
BEST SHORT FICTION: "Belsen Express," by Fritz Leiber
BEST ANTHOLOGY/COLLECTION: *The Enquiries of Dr. Eszterhazy*, by Avram Davidson
LIFE ACHIEVEMENT AWARD: Fritz Leiber

Third World Fantasy Awards (1977)
BEST NOVEL: *Doctor Rat*, by William Kotzwinkle
BEST SHORT FICTION: "There's a Long, Long Trail A-Winding," by Russell Kirk
BEST ANTHOLOGY/COLLECTION: *Frights*, edited by Kirby McCauley
LIFE ACHIEVEMENT AWARD: Ray Bradbury

Fourth World Fantasy Awards (1978)
BEST NOVEL: *Our Lady of Darkness*, by Fritz Leiber
BEST SHORT FICTION: "The Chimney," by Ramsey Campbell
BEST ANTHOLOGY/COLLECTION: *Murgunstrumm and Others*, by Hugh B. Cave
LIFE ACHIEVEMENT AWARD: Frank Belknap Long

Fifth World Fantasy Awards (1979)
BEST NOVEL: *Gloriana,* by Michael Moorcock
BEST SHORT FICTION: "Naples," by Avram Davidson
BEST ANTHOLOGY/COLLECTION: *Shadows,* edited by Charles L. Grant
LIFE ACHIEVEMENT AWARD: Jorge Luis Borges

Sixth World Fantasy Awards (1980)
BEST NOVEL: *Watchtower,* by Elizabeth A. Lynn
BEST SHORT FICTION: "The Woman Who Loved the Moon," by Elizabeth A. Lynn
Tied with: "Macintosh Willy," by Ramsey Campbell
BEST ANTHOLOGY/COLLECTION: *Amazons!,* edited by Jessica Amanda Salmonson
LIFE ACHIEVEMENT AWARD: Manly Wade Wellman

Seventh World Fantasy Awards (1981)
BEST NOVEL: *The Shadow Of The Torturer,* by Gene Wolfe
BEST SHORT FICTION: "The Ugly Chickens," by Howard Waldrop
BEST ANTHOLOGY/COLLECTION: Dark Forces, edited by Kirby McCauley
LIFE ACHIEVEMENT AWARDS: C. L. Moore

THE BRITISH FANTASY AWARDS
The British Fantasy Award, until 1976 called the August Derleth Fantasy Award, is given each year by the British Fantasy Society at FantasyCon. Originally the awards were dated for the year of bestowal (i.e., the 1972 awards were for books published in 1971), but in 1976 the system was reorganized so that the dating was based on year of publication. That is why there are two sets of awards dated 1976.

The authors extend their thanks to Karl Edward Wagner for his kindness in providing information on the British Fantasy Awards.

1972
NOVEL: *The Knight of the Swords,* by Michael Moorcock

1973
NOVEL: *The King of the Swords,* by Michael Moorcock
SHORT STORY: "The Fallible Fiend," by L. Sprague de Camp

1974
NOVEL: *Hrolf Kraki's Saga,* by Poul Anderson
SHORT STORY: "The Jade Man's Eyes," by Michael Moorcock

1975
NOVEL: *The Sword and the Stallion,* by Michael Moorcock
SHORT STORY: "Sticks," by Karl Edward Wagner

1976
NOVEL: *The Hollow Lands,* by Michael Moorcock
SHORT STORY: *The Second Book of Fritz Leiber,* by Fritz Leiber (An attempt to create a separate anthology category failed, while several stories in this book were nominated for the short-story award. The judges determined, under the circumstances, that the short-story award should go to the entire collection.)

1976
NOVEL: *The Dragon and the George,* by Gordon Dickson
SHORT STORY: "Two Suns Setting," by Karl Edward Wagner

1977
NOVEL: *A Spell for Chameleon,* by Piers Anthony
SHORT STORY: "In the Bag," by Ramsey Campbell

1978
NOVEL: The Chronicles of Thomas Covenant the Unbeliever, by Stephen R. Donaldson (The entire trilogy was published simultaneously, and was treated as a single book.)
SHORT STORY: "Jeffty Is Five," by Harlan Ellison

1979
NOVEL: *Death's Master*, by Tanith Lee
SHORT FICTION: "The Button Molder," by Fritz Leiber

1980
NOVEL: *To Wake the Dead*, by Ramsey Campbell
SHORT FICTION: "Stains," by Robert Aickman

CHAPTER SIX

Who Goes
to the Wood
beyond the World . . .

"Who goes to the wood, goes to his mother," someone once said, but who goes to the Wood beyond the World doesn't find anything so safe. William Morris's novel *The Wood Beyond the World* is generally agreed upon as being the first novel of fantasy, and even that amount of agreement is rare for those who explore that wood, who go "beyond the fields we know," as Lord Dunsany would have it, or who enter Poul Anderson's "realms of Faerie."

Morris's Wood has by now grown into a veritable forest, a trackless waste for many who venture in. Its boundaries are unsure—it tends to fade into other areas with no discernible demarcations. And though we've taken that particular Wood of 1894 as a starting point, that might be considered more for convenience than accuracy; the ancestors of this Wood go back as far as the tales told around fires in the caves, when a story was told that went beyond the ordinary "how I spent my day hunting the mammoth," but was still not an instructive fable created to explain or please the gods. The former became reportage, the latter theology. But when a tall tale was told for its own sake, that was fantasy.

But even the word fantasy compounds confusion. Nowadays it has many meanings, from erotic imaginings to a musical form. It must be read in context to make any sense at all. What *is* the context that we are using here? Perhaps, in these few pages, we may be able to answer that, to lay a few tentative paths through this strange and beautiful Wood.

But first we might check out the perimeters to see where fantasy stops and other things begin. After all, all fiction is fantasy, no matter how realistic. Madame Bovary is as much a creature of the imagination as any witch or elf, and though Claudius was once a real person, the details of his life as told by Robert Graves are more created (admittedly knowledgeably) than researched.

So fantasy is fiction wherein the people, places, and/or events are impossible or at least downright improbable—or, in a very few special cases, reality is simply changed, as in *Islandia*, where nothing impossible happens but the country of Islandia itself.

That still leaves us with a large body of literature to sort through, and this is where the vocabulary breaks down, since many allegories and satires are certainly fantasies, but for the most part have been left out of these pages. But the distinction here is fairly simply put: allegories and satires are created for a purpose aside from the story they may tell. Orwell's *Animal Farm* and Bunyan's *Pilgrim's Progress* exist on at least two levels, and the narrative—the story itself—is the lesser of these. This also means that there's little expended to make the story and its fantasy convincingly real.

So now we're down to a certain kind of fantasy which is told for its own sake and which attempts to convince the reader that the unlikely or improbable or impossible matters being narrated are true—at least for the duration of the reading of the story. (We might note here that this air of reality and conviction is one of the challenges for the writer of fantasy, and that a highly stylized manner of writing can more often than not work against this quality. This is why fantasy may be the last refuge of the honest-to-goodness storyteller.)

Can we subdivide this literature any further? Hang in there, reader; one more breakdown and then we'll leave well enough alone. Fantasy literature as defined above, which we might call "coherent fantasy" or (delicious paradox) "realistic fantasy," comes in three main flavors.

When the fantasy elements are given a scientific or pseudoscientific rationale, you've got science fiction. When they're evoked to terrify or horrify, you have the classic ghost story or tale of the supernatural. And when it's neither, you have the rarest of the subgenres, that which could be called pure fantasy. It's epitomized by Tolkien's stories of Middle-Earth, and it's mainly what we're concerned with in this volume, though we've also included those tales of the supernatural that are most appealing to fantasy lovers.

Needless to say, none of these categories is absolute. There are hybrids and overlaps, there are allegories that work so well on the narrative level that they're classics of fantasy, there are fantasies that have science-fictional elements in them, there are science-fiction horror stories (the movies particularly like these), and so on ad infinitum. And with the growing popularity of fantasy, there's an equally expanding area of science fiction with many of the qualities of pure fantasy, such as Anne McCaffrey's "Dragonrider" trilogies and Marion Bradley's "Darkover" series.

Now that certain vague boundaries have been established for the Wood, we might beat our way into the interior for a look around. Somehow a history of fantasy seems inappropriate, too cut, dried, scientific. It lends itself more to patterns, as does magic. What are the patterns of the Wood?

From our point in time, there is certainly a central pattern, centrally located in time between us and the 1890s, chosen as an arbitrary beginning. In the darkest decades of this century, the poverty-stricken 1930s and the war-torn 1940s, fantasy was at its lowest ebb, confined to children's books, whimsy, pulp magazines, and Hollywood's idea of reality (curiously inexplicable, when you consider how desperately escapism was needed during those times).

But that central pattern emerges then, and it is wonderfully symmetrical. Six writers began to publish in that period (two of them a bit earlier, in point of fact, but they reached their heyday in the thirties), who had inherited, one way or another, the major lines of fantasy of the past and who were to influence, one way or another, most of the writers to follow. They fall into sets of three, those of each set being close friends with one another. One group is Anglo-Irish, the other American.

Of the six, the two that are the central figures of their respective groups will become the major figures of fantasy in this century through the extraordinary originality of their concepts, but the other four will be remembered with only slightly less acclaim for the same reason. And each set has, already, a group appellation.

The Anglo-Irish group was the Inklings: J. R. R. Tolkien, C. S. Lewis, and Charles Williams. "The Three Musketeers of *Weird Tales*" were the Americans: Robert E. Howard, H. P. Lovecraft, and Clark Ashton Smith.

The Inklings was an informal group of students and Dons who gathered at Oxford. There were others besides the three, but theirs were the major voices to emerge. And of the three, Tolkien took the longest to become known. Williams hit his stride earliest as a novelist; Lewis became highly involved in theology, and his relatively few works of fiction reflect that involvement. The latter two, it is significant to note, wrote works using elements of the legends of King Arthur, a mine that was to be worked by many (some think too many, at this point) after them.

Tolkien, until the middle of the century, had published only a few nonacademic works, and they were considered to be for children. But in 1954 there appeared the first of a massive trilogy of books that were essentially a sequel to, and laid in the same mythological world, Middle-Earth, as his earlier work, *The Hobbit*. While this first volume, *The Fellowship of the Ring*, did not exactly hit the best-seller lists, it was not published in complete obscurity, being greeted with a full-page review in *The New York Times Book Review* by W. H. Auden.

Nevertheless, only a comparative few knew the "Middle-Earth" books for about a decade, but it seems that those few felt very strongly about them and did a good deal of proselytizing. Suddenly, in the mid-1960s, it seemed that everyone under thirty was reading them (somewhat to the dismay of those who had discovered them earlier). Subsequently, they have become classics of our time, and Tolkien's third work on Middle-Earth, published posthumously and named *The Silmarillion*, shot immediately to the top of the best-seller lists.

A good deal less fame went to the American trio, especially during their lifetimes, and it is particularly tragic that two were short-lived. (Lovecraft died at forty-seven; Howard killed himself at thirty on learning his mother was dying.)

Thanks to a literate but non-literati public, America early in this century was a breeding ground for popular fiction magazines. These had been devoted to all kinds of fiction, but about 1920 they began to specialize; the first to specialize in fantasy was *Weird Tales*. At that point, anything from occult stories to science fiction was "weird," so the magazine ran the gamut of the various subgenres.

Soon after *Weird Tales* began publishing, there appeared in it a story by a young Texan, Robert E. Howard, and another by a slightly older New Englander, Howard Phillips Lovecraft. Some years later, a young poet and artist began contributing to the magazine; he was Clark Ashton Smith, a native Californian. These three became the "Three Musketeers of *Weird Tales*," and their locative pattern is just the opposite of the three Inklings. Whereas the English became associated by being in the same place (Oxford) at the same time, the Three Musketeers' relationship came from *publishing* in the same place at the same time. They couldn't have been more scattered across the vastness of the U.S., and they never physically met; their acquaintance was only by mail, the wordage count of which may well have equaled or surpassed that of their published work.

And where the English trio made heavy use of traditional myth and religion and folklore, the Americans were making up their own; it was obvious that the Americans felt the weight of the past much less.

Howard's major contribution to fantasy was the barbarian hero ("How typically American," the English might have commented). In a culture where the frontier was not that far behind in time and civilized values were still rather new, the worlds that he created (often a mythological prehistoric Earth) were young and brawling, in which civilization almost inevitably meant decadence and evil.

Lovecraft, befitting his New England heritage, was somewhat more pro-culture; in his works, evil was often perpetrated by squalid backwoods types. He began working in the classic framework of the supernatural tale, but since he was also aware of at least the more popular aspects of science (having grown up in the period when the American belief in technology was absolute), he would justify his supernatural manifestations of evil with some sort of pseudoscientific concepts. This led to an entire cosmography of creatures from other times or "other places" (outer space or other dimensions) who wanted to wipe out mankind and take over the Earth. Anything from "out there" meant no good; Lovecraft, in his xenophobia, was expressing the classic Yankee isolationism.

Smith was to a degree the least conceptually innovative of the three, but he refined certain of their ideas and brought a sense of style to bear on his writing which was new to the pulp magazine. Howard's style was primitive and Lovecraft's purple to the point of ostentation; Smith's, while it would hardly be used as a model in a college literature course, showed a poet's sensibilities.

It's tempting to say that that double triangle was all there was in that central period, but there were indeed other wild talents around, too, at least one or two of which might be as influential. There was the roguish T. H. White, whose comically anachronistic retelling of the Arthur saga hid profound sweetness and tragedy and probably sparked the flood of Arthurian tales we are currently subjected to. There was the totally American Thorne Smith, who took whimsically fantastical ideas, presented them with supersophistication for the time, and hit best-sellerdom.

And toward the end of that dour double decade, another painter-poet, English this time, published a novel that he called "Gothic." Mervyn Peake's *Titus Groan* and its sequels may in the longest run be considered the most original of all; their profound influence on a generation that grew up on them is just beginning to be felt.

We are neglecting by name in this section, also, other writers who opened new pathways in *Weird Tales* and its fellow lowly pulps, and writers of children's tales who opened young minds to the joy of fantasy. But one phenomenon must be mentioned; it is a legendary magazine that published from 1939 to 1943 and then became a casualty of the wartime paper shortage. It was called *Unknown*, later *Unknown Worlds*, and was edited by John W. Campbell, who was in the process at that point of totally revamping science fiction with his magazine, *Astounding*. There were several magazines then devoted to s-f, and *Weird Tales* was covering the supernatural front, but that left a gap to be filled, for that elusive in-between, pure fantasy. Into that gap Campbell thrust *Unknown*.

For much of the material it published he turned to his amazing stable of young science-fiction writers, and they responded nobly, contributing stories that did for fantasy what they were doing for s-f, bringing to it clarity, logic, able writing, and an avoidance of simple formulas. And while not all the stories in *Unknown* were humorous, there was a prevailing light tone that matched the general whimsy to which fantasy of the time, in books and films, was prone.

It was for *Unknown* that Williamson, Bester, Van Vogt, and even Heinlein wrote fantasies; probably the most successful of all were those of Theodore Sturgeon, with, for instance, the memorable "It," and of L. Sprague de Camp, whose collaborations with Fletcher Pratt literally brought an entire new dimension to fantasy, and Fritz Leiber, who satirized a whole subgenre before it existed, with his Gray Mouser stories. Those particular three, whose careers were just beginning then, went on to become notable in science fiction *and* fantasy, a sort of second-generation triad and another triangle for our pattern. (And, to link the two American threesomes, de Camp has done a detailed and readable biography of Lovecraft.)

The time, the authors, and the magazines we have just talked about form a sort of nexus, the manageable neck of an hourglass pattern, with innumerable threads leading into it, and even more leading out into our own day and age.

Of the great predecessors, we might note those who wielded the most influence from the nineteenth and early twentieth centuries, without becoming too historical about it. The lines of influence sometimes lead in unexpected directions and weave an oddly tangled web. For instance, because America of the last century was not exactly noted for the breadth of its literary spectrum—what good writing was done was done within very narrow limits, which did not include fantasy (with one important exception)—the English were major influences on the Three Musketeers. Perhaps that would be best corrected to Irish, since the jeweled exoticism of Dunsany and Wilde certainly flavor Howard and Smith, and even the early Lovecraft, whose only real novel, *The Dream Quest of Unknown Kadath*, is extraordinarily Dunsanian, not excepting a few ghouls here and there. Howard also, with his penchant toward action and adventure, swordplay, and lost civilizations, looked through Edgar Rice Burroughs to H. Rider Haggard. It might be noted that Burroughs had created a hero from the wild in Tarzan, who in turn was certainly fathered by Kipling's Mowgli. From there it was but a step to Howard's barbarian Conan and his clones (and Leiber's laughing tribute in Fafhrd, companion to the Gray Mouser).

The important American exception mentioned above is, of course, Edgar Allan Poe, but the hiatus between his death in 1849, which brought a sort of temporary dead-end to the American horror story, and the rise of the twentieth-century American fantasists made his influence distant. Though Lovecraft, in particular, is called "the successor to Poe," it is more because he is an American writer of horror tales than for any real similarity in their style or approach.

The Inklings took very different sources; the threads that tie them to the past end in very different places, many of which have the flavor of childhood (but *not*, by any means, childishness). They eschewed the gun-toting, assagai-wielding action of Haggard and the hothouse glamor of Dunsany for the less sophisticated, gentler fairy-tale fantasies of MacDonald and the medieval glamor (in the old sense of *magic*) of William Morris (and we've come back here to his *The Wood Beyond the World* by a most roundabout path). And another source, perhaps the most important and least known of all, was the children's stories of Edith Nesbit, with their determined logic and sense of the reality of magic, as opposed to the surrealist phantasmagorias of MacDonald's adult tales and Carroll's Alice books.

And farther and farther back, there are the folk tales, especially of Britain, and especially of Arthur, but also Germanic and Norse and Celtic, all the rich heritage of England and Ireland. And the magic rings, talking birds, and dragons of Wagner's operas; and the nature spirits, dryads, and wilis and ondines of the entire European Romantic Age. And even farther back, the mythology and theology of Christianity and other religions too.

Out of all this the Anglo-Irish writers wove tales of beauty, majesty, and magic, where the Americans, befitting their raw and polyglot culture, made up their own worlds and mythologies based on raw emotions of courage and fear. Who is to say which is the better or more creative?

(We might note that our patterning has to a degree neglected the ghost stories and tales of the supernatural. They have their own history and their own patterns, from the fearsome bogies invented to frighten children around the cave- and camp-fires through the gothic novel and the perfect miniatures of M. R. James to the occult nastinesses of Stephen King's novels.)

What patterns do we find on this side of our nexus? What has the Wood grown into?

Dear reader, this entire book is devoted to showing you that pattern, the incredibly rich mosaic that fantasy has become. We truly live in a Golden Age of fantasy, and its rewards and fairies can keep an avid reader busy for a lifetime. Why this leafing and branching, this verdant fecundity in barely a decade or two?

For an answer, we can but point to those six authors again. Each, in his way, pushed the borders of fantasy farther beyond the fields we know. Each captured the imagination of several generations, and Tolkien and Howard in particular touched some vital, even primal wellspring of need to enlarge the horizons of the mundane. As their books were published and reprinted, as enthusiastic readers pushed them on friends, as the 1960s changed our culture to one which allowed dreams that were not directly practical, functional, or salable, young writers more and more chose to write *this* kind of story. And these dreams sold.

A new term was coined to describe the plethora of Conanesque thud-and-blunderers, "sword-and-sorcery." But it was difficult to make any real distinction between that and the Tolkienesque, and as sword-and-sorcery became more and more a pejorative epithet, "heroic fantasy" became the alternative and more acceptable descriptive phrase.

But while that subgenre became the mainstream of fantasy, other areas of the Wood were reexplored or trailblazed, from the elves of *A Midsummer Night's Dream,* revisited in Linda Haldeman's *The Lastborn of Elvinwood,* to the halls of Gormenghast, paid tribute to in Moorcock's *Gloriana.* And even fantasy's thriving little brother, science fiction, who had seemed likely to take over the whole genre, began to take on more and more of the trappings of fantasy, as in Silverberg's *Lord Valentine's Castle* and Wolfe's "Book of the New Sun" tetralogy.

What of the future? The patterns will change, grow, shrink, and recombine; practical ages will come and go, and dreamers' ages will come and go. But woe to humanity if the environment of the Wood beyond the World becomes so polluted that it becomes a wasteland. Then indeed we will be another species, and a lesser one.

AUTHORS' NOTE: A crystal ball could tell us of the wonderful writers and works that will inevitably emerge after this book is finished. Since none of our collective talents include crystallomancy, we can but state our regrets while still hoping that there will be many, many such.

Winner of the HUGO AWARD
for the Best All Time Science Fiction Series
JAMES BLISH

JACK OF EAGLES   61150-3/$2.75
A fast-paced science fiction-ESP novel, first published in the
1950's and now considered a classic, in which an average New
York copywriter suddenly realizes that he has ESP, and is
plunged into a dangerous world of madmen bent on world
domination.

DOCTOR MIRABILIS   60335-7/$2.95
In this classic novel, Blish vividly captures the life of Roger
Bacon, the brilliant and eccentric philosopher whose radical
teachings and heretical scientific theories led to his persecu-
tion at the hands of the 13th century Catholic Church.

BLACK EASTER   59568-0/$2.50
Theron Ware, the black magician and most satanic wizard on
Earth, is told to unleash the demons of Hell, just for one
evening. But when all Hell breaks loose, Earth becomes the
site of the most unimaginable horror...

THE DAY AFTER JUDGMENT   59527-3/$2.50
The powerful sequel to BLACK EASTER, in which the sur-
vivors of World War III awake to find Satan ruling the Earth,
and become caught in the ultimate battle between good and
evil.

CITIES IN FLIGHT   58602-9/$3.50
AT LAST THE FOUR NOVELS IN ONE VOLUME!
A perennial best-seller, CITIES IN FLIGHT is a science
fiction classic. In this tetralogy, the author has structured an
entire universe in which mankind is no longer bound to the
solar system, but has become both conqueror and victim of
the stars.

THE STAR DWELLERS   57976-6/$1.95
When a life form as old as the universe is discovered, its
tremendous energy could be of great use on Earth, and man is
faced, for the first time, with the implications of trusting an
alien creature.